WITHDRAWN

Handbook for Learning Mentors in Primary and Secondary Schools

Handbook for Learning Mentors in Primary and Secondary Schools

MARGARET ROBERTS AND DOT CONSTABLE

David Fulton Publishers

London

David Fulton Publishers Ltd
The Chiswick Centre, 414 Chiswick High Road, London W4 5TF
www.fultonpublishers.co.uk

David Fulton Publishers is a division of Granada Learning Ltd, part of the Granada Media group

First published 2003
10 9 8 7 6 5 4 3 2 1

British Library Cataloguing in Publication Data
A catalogue record for this book is available from the British Library.

ISBN 1–85346–980–7

Typeset by Book Production Services, London
Printed and bound in Great Britain by Ashford Colour Press Limited, Gosport, Hants

Contents

Acknowledgements

As the authors of this book we would like to take this opportunity to thank and acknowledge the large number of people that have afforded us their time, support and energy in providing information, ideas and sharing of practice.

As we embarked on the task of putting this work together we were encouraged from the outset by the enthusiasm that we were met with by all who have involvement with Learning Mentors. As we progressed into the work of the mentors themselves we were equally if not more impressed. It has to be said that after some of the meetings with particular mentors we were left feeling exhausted after their descriptions of a 'normal' working day.

While gathering information, writing, re-drafting, rewriting we have had contact with mentors, schools, Connexions and LEAs. There have been telephone calls, emails and visits and we would like to thank all of those who helped us. We realise that to name everyone that we have encountered would be unrealistic but we would like to give special mention to those who have in some way or other made a major contribution to our work. We would like to send our heartfelt thanks to the following people, their schools and their local education authorities for their valued support throughout:

Julia Tortise, Link Learning Mentor (Secondary) and Nicola Winwood, Link Learning Mentor (Primary), Birmingham LEA

Sarah Stokoe, Link Learning Mentor, Doncaster

Robbie Holmes, Learning Mentor, Brookfield High School, Kirkby, Knowsley

Fiona Scanlan, Development Manager, Connexions, Northfield, Birmingham

Sharon Westhead, Learning Mentor, Croxteth Community Comprehensive School, Liverpool

Denise Fox, Learning Mentor, Deykin Avenue Junior and Infant School, Birmingham

Maggie Aylott, Deputy Headteacher, and Matthew Job, Learning Mentor, Dormers Wells High School, Southall

Nicki Rees, Jenni Ralph, Debbi Whyborn, Graeme Phillips and Laura Coe, Learning Mentors, Kings Norton High School, part of the Kings Norton Education Action Zone (KNEAZ), Birmingham

Joan Eastman , Pupil Support Manager , Ninestiles Technology College, Birmingham

Jackie Ranger, Student Support Co-ordinator, Perry Beeches School, Birmingham

Julia Baker, Lead Learning Mentor for Peer Mentoring and Study Skills, Sheffield Support, Teaching and Education Psychology Service

Ginny Joyce, Learning Mentor, Shireland Language College, Sandwell

Isabella Ellis, Learning Mentor, Wilkes Green Infant School, Birmingham

Introduction

What is a Learning Mentor?

> Helping young people overcome barriers to learning through one-to-one mentoring, regular contact with families/carers and encouraging positive family involvement.

This definition can be found on the DfES Standards website under Excellence in Cities – Learning Mentors. Well, it's easy then, a straightforward explanation setting out what a Learning Mentor does, but what if you want to know more?

Well, further research will soon lead to other documents that give varying explanations of the role of the mentor, what tasks they should be involved in and how they can impact on learning. However, if you are looking for guidance on understanding the role in relation to actually carrying out the work, this will provide a more serious challenge. There is a definite need for a more practical guide that provides an insight into the working life of a Learning Mentor on a day-to-day basis – warts and all!

For those mentors coming into the role from outside the education field the reality of daily life in a school can be somewhat of a shock. Everyone has attended school and will have their own preconceived ideas about school life, their favourite teachers, their worst experiences, their successes and failures. Working inside a school as an employee rather than the customer will be vastly different. The mentor needs to have an idea of what working in a school is all about, and that is just the start. Once understanding of a particular school's structure and systems is established, working within them becomes the next issue. Add to that the actual job of mentoring the pupils and you have a real task on your hands.

How can this book help?

Well, hopefully the introduction so far has not frightened off any prospective Learning Mentors or indeed made those already in post think twice about their job. If that is the case, don't give up just yet – help is most definitely at hand. In addition to providing information on your purpose and role within the school, this book will provide information, ideas, strategies and support materials for your daily life in school. It is intended to be used both for reference and practical application purposes and, with this in mind, many of the materials have been put together with a view to being a resource bank for the Learning Mentor.

This publication may also be of interest to

Headteachers
Senior Management Teams
Training Providers for Learning Mentors
LEA Advisers involved in School Improvement
Teachers in Schools working with Learning Mentors

The layout of the book is intended to provide an easily accessible resource that may be read as a whole or in part to support the Learning Mentor and all of those involved and interested in their effective practice in schools.

1 The role of the mentor in relation to learning

Definition of a mentor?

The most common explanation given to children usually involves telling the tale of Odysseus who chose Mentor, a 'true and trusted' friend, to act as a guide and adviser to his son when he went off to fight wars. To use this as a definition of mentoring however, both undervalues and underestimates the contribution that mentors make to learning by young people.

Dictionary definitions give us words like consultant, counsellor, advice-giver, guru. We could look at many more definitions/explanations but taking the essence of them all, we could perhaps say that mentoring is about one person offering support to another through establishing a relationship and supporting their development, learning and growth. With this explanation in mind, let us consider what this may mean in relation to children.

Support for learning

'Sorry I'm late, I've been to see my mentor.' Sharon entered the classroom noisily and sat down. The teacher and other pupils largely ignored her; they were used to this as it happened each week. Sharon had a regular appointment with her Learning Mentor at this time, and despite pleas from her teacher it had apparently been deemed impossible for the appointment to be rearranged so that Sharon did not always miss her French lesson. Sharon was delighted with the situation as she disliked French.

The above exchange highlights some of the tensions and misunderstandings that can exist in schools with regard to support for learning. The school is a good one, with caring staff, but the pupils perceived that mentors only worked with youngsters who had problems. Furthermore, the teacher was not too certain why Sharon had this appointment so she did not get openly involved in a debate about her lateness, but she had spoken to the Learning Mentor to express her concern that Sharon was regularly missing the lesson. Far from 'removing barriers to learning', the Learning Mentor was creating extra ones.

Thankfully, in the main, such misunderstandings are a thing of the past and Learning Mentors are now accepted as respected professionals in areas that have the benefit of being part of the Excellence in Cities programme.

Learning Mentors are one of an ever-growing band of adults who are supporting the learning of young people in our schools. Their title relates to the Excellence in Cities initiative, but a variety of appointments with similar responsibilities have been made in schools in other areas. They are tasked with 'removing barriers to learning'. Learning Support Assistants also work with pupils who have identified learning difficulties and additionally support the work of teachers. Adult volunteer mentors exist in their thousands and give freely of their time to support youngsters in schools and help them to overcome problems which get in the way of their learning. It is perhaps little wonder that staff and pupils sometimes get confused about the respective roles of all of these adults.

In order to have a clear picture of what impact each of these roles may have on the development and learning of children there is a need for a deeper understanding of the roles so that the Learning Mentor may see where they 'fit' into the wider picture of whole school learning support.

The Learning Support Assistant (LSA)

Learning Support Assistants are an invaluable asset to any school. There are a range of titles schools may use to describe such personnel, for example, Teaching Assistant, Classroom Assistant, Non-Teaching Assistant, Special Needs Assistant, Nursery Nurse. Irrespective of the title allocated, they will all have one thing in common, they will be employed by the schools and have a clearly defined role that is negotiated with the school's Special Needs Co-ordinator (SENCO) or Inclusion Co-ordinator. Their job is to work with individuals or small groups of pupils with the aim of enhancing their learning.

To fulfil the role their aim is to enable the pupils to participate fully in the social and academic life of the school by supporting the teaching staff in the delivery of the curriculum. By adopting a range of strategies, the LSA works towards encouraging pupils to become independent learners. The LSA will work with the class teacher to produce materials and resources which are appropriate and that take into account the particular needs of the pupil(s) with whom they are working. In addition, they often work alongside the pupils in the classroom and help to ensure that they stay 'on task'. An important part of their role is to provide feedback to the class teacher on the success or otherwise of strategies being used. This is particularly important in primary schools, where LSAs have a key role to play in supporting work undertaken during literacy and numeracy hour.

It is likely the actual day-to-day work of the LSA, in the first instance, will be dictated by Individual Education Plans. Some LSAs may specialise and have expert knowledge, on autism or hearing impairment for example, thus enabling them to advise the class teacher about the appropriateness or otherwise of the strategies they are adopting. This is equally the case when working with pupils who have identified behavioural difficulties such as Attention Deficit Hyperactivity Disorder (ADHD). Their role is that of adviser supporter. Through their dedicated work they are able to enable pupils to stay in mainstream classrooms – an important factor when schools consider their inclusion agenda.

The greatest issue for an LSA can often be that of their contract of employment. It may be linked to the funding of statemented pupils and thus, should the statement cease for any reason, or if the child moves on from the school, the funding will cease and so will their employment.

Bilingual Teaching Assistants

Bilingual Teaching Assistants may work alongside pupils for whom English is an additional language. They are uniquely well placed to offer support in the classroom, enabling pupils to feel part of the class and being included, with support, in all activities. Such inclusion provides an effective means of acquiring certain skills; however, it has also been shown that some things can be more readily learnt if the pupils are able to have opportunities to use their first language while they are learning English. The Bilingual Teaching Assistant is able to allow this to happen. This type of support also enables the pupils to build on prior knowledge and experience, thus supporting their learning. During any assessment of the pupils' abilities or aptitudes, the Teaching Assistant can provide an important link to ensure mutual understanding and therefore allow more accurate assessment results to be obtained. Even when bilingual assistants do not speak the home language of particular pupils, they will have an insight into how language works, the importance of home–school links and the need for cultural sensitivity. In light of this an important contribution associated with their role is that of communicator for both pupils and parents where there may be a need to explain the education processes of the United Kingdom and its requirements.

Personal Advisers

The careers service has always provided support to youngsters, and in fact has an obligation to provide advice to youngsters from year 8 onwards. The advent of the Personal Advisers of the Connexions service has added a further level of support to youngsters but also has the potential for adding to the confusion about services on offer.

It is envisaged that when the Connexions service is fully operational all young people in the 13–19 age group in England will have access to a Personal Adviser. For some young people this will merely be for careers advice, but for others it may involve in-depth support to help identify barriers to learning and find solutions. Much of this work will involve one-to-one support and guidance, especially at the key times of transition, e.g. Key Stage 4 and post-16, or when decisions have to be made which will affect their future education and training. The advisers have a duty to work also with parents, carers and the families of the young people.

Pupils who need more personal support, e.g. 'those at risk of not participating effectively in education and training', will have support that could include one-to-one mentoring, group or peer support and personal development activities. This could further involve referral to specialists in and outside the school.

3

Mentors

Mentors come in a range of guises! In order to gain some perspective of the range of mentoring going on in schools, consider one secondary school visited recently, which, had the following schemes in operation:

- Peer mentoring whereby pupils in year 9 were supporting year 6 pupils in local primary schools and then continued this support when the primary pupils moved into the secondary school. As well as the obvious advantages of making both groups of pupils feel supported and wanted, the school had increased its year 7 intake as a consequence of the peer mentoring programme.
- Volunteer business mentors were working in the technology and business studies departments of the school. They offered expertise in their subject areas, arranged visits to businesses, arranged work experience placements and helped pupils with mock interviews and completion of application forms.
- Players from a local football team (first division) came and assisted with PE lessons, helped with after school clubs and undertook some one-to-one mentoring. They became role models for many of the youngsters and gave them something to which they could aspire.
- Representatives from the African-Caribbean community mentored underachieving African-Caribbean pupils. They worked closely with the pupils and their families and had a good degree of success. One of the few problems that emerged was how to explain to the mentees why their white friends could not join the sessions!
- Mentors who had themselves been in care supported two youngsters who were in care.
- Members of the senior management team mentored pupils whose attendance fell below 80 per cent and as a consequence their attendance improved and their families also began to understand the importance of regular attendance.
- Teachers mentored year 11 pupils, and helped raise their aspirations with regard to target GCSE grades.
- Learning Mentors supported pupils in Key Stage 3 and helped minimise the effects of 'barriers to learning'.

All of the mentors were actively engaged in working with the pupils for a variety of reasons. There is, however, a need to understand the differences between volunteer mentors and Learning Mentors who are employed by the schools with a working role defined by the Excellence in Cities initiative.

Volunteer mentors

Each mentoring experience is unique, reflecting the experience and skills of both mentor and mentee. Both the mentor and mentee will have different expectations of the mentoring process, and it is expected that both parties will benefit. There is a further expectation that the institution to which the mentee belongs will also benefit, as will the mentor's organization in the case of business mentors. A consideration of some volunteer mentoring programmes that are operating in schools may serve to demonstrate some of these benefits. Volunteer mentors are not part of the school organisation and their work is usually co-ordinated by an external body to which they are accountable. They will all have received training prior to undertaking any mentoring, and as with all who work with young people police checks will have been undertaken to ensure that there is no reason why they should not work with young people in schools.

Business Mentors

Business Mentors tend to participate in a variety of schemes run by Education Business Partnerships. They typically work with a year 10 or 11 pupil in the build-up to GCSE examinations. Their objective is usually to help pupils develop the confidence and motivation needed to ensure success at GCSE and to help equip them for the decisions they will need to take about entering the world of work or further training. They may further contribute to the curriculum of the school by offering support in their areas of expertise, and help with mock interviews, careers conventions and the like. In return, the business has a role in influencing the standard of the future workforce, has an improved understanding of the local community, increases the company's profile in the community and extends opportunities for the personal and professional development of its employees.

Community Mentors

Community Mentors have many roles. Some belong to a minority ethnic group and offer support to the same group. Several African-Caribbean mentor groups exist, for example, and have the specific aim of supporting African-Caribbean young people and their families, and enabling the youngsters to achieve their potential. In this they are usually very successful as they are able to empathise with the young people, help to develop their self-esteem and act as role models. They have the respect of the communities in which they work, and can act as intermediaries between home and school as needed. Other community groups including several church groups also contribute to mentoring in schools. Such groups often work with pupils who need to develop their social-personal skills, or who are at risk of exclusion. The pupils need the support of an adult from outside the school who will listen to them and be non-judgemental. One mentee described her mentor as someone to whom she could 'ask questions you can't ask your parents or your teachers because you would get into trouble'.

Intergenerational mentoring

Intergenerational mentoring schemes acknowledge the experience of the older generation and the special support that they can offer young people. They have a lifetime of experience to share with youngsters, and time to give. In turn, mentoring can provide the mentor with a sense of achievement and the personal satisfaction of feeling needed and valued by the community.

University student mentors

University students also have a part to play in mentoring young people. Some are used as role models and they are able to share their experiences with youngsters and support those aspiring to a university education. Others, having experienced success themselves, want to motivate underachieving youngsters and those who are at risk of exclusion and offer them the encouragement they need to succeed.

Mentors with specialist knowledge

Mentors who have a specialist knowledge can make a very valuable contribution, for example, hearing impaired mentors working with mentees who have a hearing impairment; or mentors who have been in public care, working with mentees who are in public care. In this type of situation, the mentor is able to empathise with the particular situation of their mentee and thus offer another dimension to the relationship.

Whatever the nature of such voluntary mentoring, when successful, the benefits are clear. The mentee has improved self-confidence and self-esteem, increased motivation, broader horizons and raised aspiration and attainment. The mentor has developed a range of skills, has greater understanding, feels valued and has been able to give something back to the community. Schools have a range of benefits, which include more positive pupils, improved attendance, improved attainment and possibly a reduction in exclusions. Businesses have access to professional development opportunities and a higher profile within the community. All in all, everyone is able to gain something.

So, we must now ask ourselves, how does the role of the Learning Mentor differ?

Learning Mentors

Learning Mentors share many of the skills of the volunteers but their role is different. They are employed by the school in which they work and their focus is to raise achievement within the formal environment of the school. Their role is defined by the Excellence in Cities programme although schools do have the flexibility to interpret aspects of the role to suit the particular context of the school. The prime role of the Learning Mentor is to assist the school in enabling pupils to overcome any barriers to learning that may contribute to their underachievement and ultimately to social exclusion. The Learning Mentor works with individual pupils using a range of strategies such as one-to-one interviewing and target-setting and small group work. Their overall aim is to enable the young person with whom they are working to fully engage within the mainstream school setting. The Learning Mentor will also provide a single point of access to additional support such as out of school study support, community and voluntary organisations, the Youth Services and the Careers/ Connexions service. Learning Mentors must therefore operate as part of a team within the school in which they are based, but also be part of a network of wider contacts outside the school.

The background of the Learning Mentor

In order to fully understand their role, it is important to acknowledge the background from which the role was created, and for what purpose.

Learning Mentors became established as part of the Excellence in Cities initiative, which was in turn part of the government's agenda to 'raise standards, tackle failure and create a new culture of opportunity and success'. The original strategy focused on six inner-city conurbations: Inner London, Birmingham, Manchester/Salford, Liverpool/Knowsley, Sheffield/Rotherham and Leeds/Bradford. The initiative has subsequently been expanded to a large number of LEAs both in cities and more recently in Excellence Clusters and now covers a wide area of the country.

In addition to the above, the role of Primary Learning Mentors is currently under development. They have the objective of helping children to overcome barriers to learning both inside and outside school to help the children thrive at school. The Primary Learning Mentors help the children at times of transition from pre-school to school; from infant to junior classes; and particularly from primary to secondary school, at which point they will work closely with the Secondary Learning Mentors to help provide continuity of support.

As you can see, within the Excellence in Cities framework, the Learning Mentor element of the initiative has had, and indeed continues to have, a huge role to play in promoting and improving the achievement of pupils across the country.

So, the next question is, how do they fulfil their role?

The job in hand!

Although the employing school decides the actual job description for the Learning Mentor, advice given by the DfES states it should include the following:

Transfer of information and assessment:
- To promote speedy and effective transfer of pupil information from primary to secondary schools in order to smooth transition.
- To participate (with teaching and other staff) in the assessment of all children entering or returning to school, and of all children at the end of years 6 and 9, in order to identify those needing extra help from a Learning Mentor to overcome barriers to learning.
- To co-ordinate individual support with the Gifted and Talented Co-ordinator and with the Special Educational Needs Co-ordinator (SENCO) to ensure complementarity.

Mentoring and support:
- To draw up and implement an action plan for each child who needs particular support (except where the child is already subject to an individually tailored plan, in which case to contribute to reviews and work towards objectives in the plan).
- To maintain regular contact with families/carers of children receiving support, and to encourage positive family involvement in the child's learning.

Signposting:
- To build up a full knowledge of the range of support available for pupils.
- To act as a single point of contact for accessing specialist support, e.g. Probation Service, Careers Service/Connexions; Social Services, out-of-school study support, and a range of community and business-based programmes.
- To liaise with post -16 Personal Advisers to identify Key Stage 4 pupils at risk of dropping out and ensure that they have an identified programme of post-compulsory training and education.

Working with voluntary mentors:
- To work closely with local community and business mentors, and take an active role in co-ordinating and supporting the work of voluntary mentors working with pupils both in and out of school, so the young person's needs are met in an integrated and focused way.

Measuring success

In order to evaluate the impact of their role, the Learning Mentor has to be able evaluate their impact on learning. In order to do this, the success or otherwise of their work may be judged by criteria laid down by the local Excellence in Cities partnership and could include, for example:

1 Improved attendance and punctuality.
2 Reduced fixed term and permanent exclusions.
3 Improved attainment especially with regard to vulnerable groups.

We can see from the above that the Learning Mentor has a much higher degree of accountability within the school than do the various volunteer mentor groups that may work within the same institution.

Where do all of these people fit in?

It is very clear that there are numerous avenues for schools to explore in relation to support for learning, and in order to establish a coherent system it is imperative that the work of these people is co-ordinated well if it is to be wholly effective. As part of this co-ordination, it would help if the school provided a chart identifying all of the personnel involved with their pupils, their roles, responsibilities and success criteria. (Table 1.1)

In addition to this, it is equally important that the personnel are informed of the organisation and working of the school; so let us take a look at school systems and structures.

Table 1.1 Support for learning

TITLE	FOCUS	REPORTING TO:	SUCCESS CRITERIA FOR PUPILS
Learning Support Assistant	In-class support Small group/ individual work Production of resources	SENCO	Curriculum accessed Socially integrated into school life
Volunteer Mentor	One-to-one talk Small group discussion Appointments made through school	Head of Pastoral Care/ Head of Year/ School Mentor Co-ordinator	Negotiated targets reached Improved self-confidence A positive view of life
Learning Mentor	Working with pupils in and out of classrooms Work outside of school hours and into school holidays	LEA Lead Learning Mentor and nominated member of school staff	Improved attendance Improved self-esteem Improved engagement in learning situations Improved levels of achievement
Connexions Personal Adviser	Individual	Connexions Service and nominated member of school staff	Personal development needs identified and addressed Targets met, e.g. attendance, improved attitude towards continuing education Reduction in exclusions

2 School systems, structures and provision

Understanding the education system

All staff working within a school should have some knowledge of how legislation and guidance impact upon their daily lives in school. In order to fully understand this, we first need to consider the hierarchical structure of our education system and the roles and responsibilities of those within it.

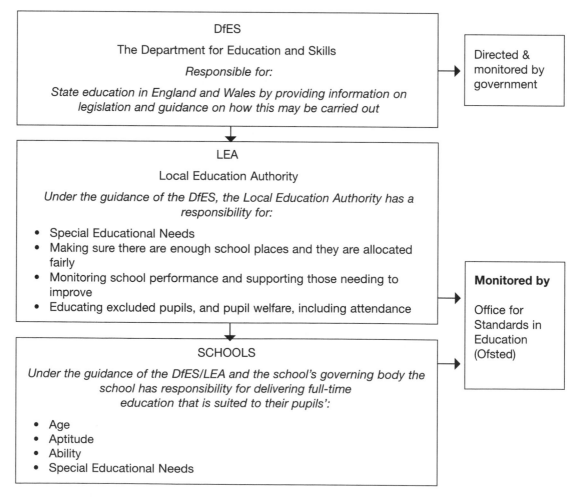

Figure 2.1 The education system

Figure 2.1 gives a very basic outline of how our system of education works. It demonstrates the flow of legislative documentation, information and instruction through to its implementation. Responsibility begins with the Department for Education and Skills (DfES), who disseminate information to local education authorities (LEAs) who in turn inform schools, who bring theory to life. As within any major organisation there has to be the facility to monitor provision. In education, at the highest level, it is the role of the government to monitor the effectiveness of the DfES. At LEA and school level, it is the role of the Office for Standards in Education (Ofsted) who evaluate the quality of all provision although the LEA has a role to play in monitoring school performance.

This very basic outline provides some small insight into what affects the day-to-day organisation and running of a school. However, in order to gain a greater understanding of how this impacts upon the children with whom we work, there is a need to examine school organisation and what schools offer to their customers – the pupils.

School organisation and provision

Education for our children is, in the main, divided into primary and secondary schools where pupils transfer from one phase to the other at the age of 11. Some local education authorities do, however, have a three-stage system where pupils move from primary at the age of 8 or 9 years to a 'middle school' and then on to secondary school at the age of 12 or 13 years. Irrespective of the school system that the child is placed into, the common theme throughout is that of the curriculum and the staffing requirements to deliver it.

Curriculum

The school curriculum comprises all the learning and other experiences that each school plans for its pupils. The Education Reform Act (1988), and the Education Act (1997) require that all state schools provide pupils with a curriculum that

- is balanced and broadly based;
- promotes their spiritual, moral, cultural, mental and physical development;
- prepares them for the opportunities, responsibilities and experiences of adult life.

The National Curriculum was introduced in 1988 by the Education Reform Act with the aim of improving standards by providing a broad and balanced curriculum for all pupils, with continuity and progressions in learning from 5 to 16. The National Curriculum does not constitute the whole curriculum of a school, so that schools are also able to respond to the particular needs of their communities. Although the National Curriculum includes statutory requirements about what is to be taught it does not dictate how subjects are to be taught, and so schools have the freedom to decide the best approaches to teaching and learning for their pupils.

Table 2.1 The National Curriculum

	Key Stage 1	Key Stage 2	Key Stage 3	Key Stage 4
Age	5–7	7 – 11	11–4	14–16
Year groups	1–2	3–6	7–9	10–11
Core subjects				
English	•	•	•	•
Mathematics	•	•	•	•
Science	•	•	•	•
Foundation subjects				
D & T	•	•	•	•
ICT	•	•	•	•
Geography	•	•	•	
History	•	•	•	
MFL	OPTIONAL	OPTIONAL	•	•
Art & Design	•	•	•	
Music	•	•	•	
PE	•	•	•	•
Citizenship	OPTIONAL	OPTIONAL	•	•

Religious Education is not a National Curriculum subject but there is a statutory requirement that all schools must provide religious education for the pupils.

Sex Education – the law requires that primary schools have a policy on sex education but there is no requirement that it be taught as a separate topic if it is provided within the curriculum, e.g. science. Secondary schools must provide sex education for their pupils.

Careers Education – provision has to be made for careers education in schools for pupils from the age of 13 (year 8/9) onwards.

PSHE and Citizenship – The National Curriculum provides guidance about PSHE and Citizenship in Key Stages 1 and 2, and many primary schools include it in their school curriculum. PSHE guidance also exists for Key Stages 3 and 4, but Citizenship is a statutory requirement. Most schools already teach PSHE as a separate subject and this includes sex education, drugs education and careers as well as themes which will become part of citizenship.

Understanding the National Curriculum

The National Curriculum is divided into four stages:

- Key Stage 1: from 5 to 7 years
- Key Stage 2: from 7 to 11 years
- Key Stage 3: from 11 to 14 years
- Key Stage 4: from 14 to 16 years

Each stage contains Core and Foundation subjects (Table 2.1), the content of which is clearly laid out in two handbooks – one for primary schools and one for secondary schools. Programmes of study indicate both the knowledge, skills and understanding that has to be covered as well as the breadth of study that is required for each subject. They further indicate descriptions of the levels of attainment or attainment targets within which pupils are expected to work at each Key Stage.

The National Curriculum handbooks further stress a requirement that teachers tailor their work to ensure that all pupils are able to access the curriculum, and this expectation is detailed in the inclusion chapter of the handbooks. In planning and teaching the National Curriculum teachers are expected to have due regard to three principles:

- Setting suitable learning challenges
- Responding to pupils' diverse learning needs
- Overcoming potential barriers to learning and assessment for individuals and groups of pupils

The purposes of the National Curriculum are fourfold:

1 To establish entitlement whereby the National Curriculum secures an entitlement to a number of areas of learning for all pupils irrespective of any social, cultural or other factors.
2 To establish standards so that national standards are set for all schools as a result of which targets can be set and performance compared between schools, groups and individuals.
3 To promote continuity and coherence which will ensure progression in pupils' learning. This also helps with transition of pupils between schools and between phases.
4 To promote public understanding and promote a common basis for discussion of education issues among lay and professional groups, including pupils, parents, teachers, governors and employers.

Other considerations

Following on from the National Curriculum, the drive to raise standards has also resulted in many new curriculum initiatives. Of these, it is perhaps the National Literacy Strategy (1998) and the National Numeracy Strategy (1999) that have had the greatest impact, and following on from their success, the Key Stage 3 Strategy:

The National Literacy Strategy

The strategy, introduced in 1998

- set challenging literacy targets
- was designed to raise the standards of literacy in primary schools in England
- provided training and support.

The National Literacy Framework for Teaching

- provided documentation to schools to support their efforts in the delivery of the strategy.

The National Numeracy Strategy

The strategy, introduced in 1999

- set challenging numeracy targets
- was designed to raise the standards of numeracy in primary schools in England
- provided training and support.

The National Numeracy Framework for Teaching Mathematics

- provided documentation to schools to support their efforts in the delivery of the strategy.

The Key Stage 3 Strategy

The strategy, introduced in 2001, was designed to:

- establish high expectations for all pupils and set challenging targets
- strengthen the transition from Key Stage 2 to Key Stage 3 to ensure progression in teaching and learning across Key Stage 3
- promote approaches to teaching and learning to engage and motivate pupils and demand their active participation
- strengthen teaching and learning through a programme of professional development and practical support.

We can see from this information that schools work within a very structured system, and this enables accountability through scrutiny of test and examination results. A school's performance is measured through Standard Attainment Tests and assessments that are built into Key Stages 1, 2 and 3 (Figure 2.2). Where Key Stage 4 is concerned, the curriculum becomes more flexible and is unique to each school (Figure 2.3). As one would expect, however, performance continues to be measured. This is done through analysis of external examination results gained at GCSE (General Certificate of Secondary Education) and GNVQ (General National Vocational Qualification) levels.

Teacher assessment is used to complement results from external tests

Key Stage 1: Expected attainment level for 7-year-olds = 2

Reading tasks levels 1–2
Reading comprehension test levels 1–2
Reading comprehension test level 3
Writing task levels 1– 3
Spelling tests levels 1–3
Mathematics tasks level 1
Mathematics tests levels 2–3

Key Stage 2: Expected attainment level for 11-year-olds = 4

Reading tests levels 3–5
Writing tests levels 3–5
Spelling/handwriting tests levels 3–5
English extension test level 6
Maths test A levels 3–5
Maths test B levels 3–5
Mental arithmetic levels 3–5
Maths extension test level 6
Science test A levels 3–5
Science test B levels 3–5
Science extension test level 6

NB: Not all year 6 children take the English test. If the teacher decides that the child is working at level 1 or 2 the child will not be entered for the test. Teacher assessment alone will be used.

Key Stage 3: Expected attainment level for 14-year-olds = 5

English – reading and writing levels 4–7
English – Shakespeare
Mathematics 1 levels 3–8
Mathematics 2
Mental arithmetic
Science 1 levels 3–8
Science 2

Extension papers are available for pupils working at level 8 or who show exceptional performance. Teacher assessment is the only assessment requirement for pupils who have been working at level 3 or below in English or level 2 or below in maths and science.

Teacher assessment is required in the following subjects:

English	Maths	Science	Modern Foreign Language	Geography	Citizenship
History	ICT	Art	Design & Technology	Music	PE

These assessments complement the SATs and allow judgement of pupil performance over a period of time.

In addition, progress tests are set at the end of year 7 for pupils who did not reach level 4 in their year 6 SATs. Half-termly Literacy Progress Units are available for pupils who enter year 7 at level 3.

Figure 2.2 Standard Assessment Tests (SATs) – national tests

ENGLISH   MATHEMATICS   SCIENCE

INFORMATION COMMUNICATION TECHNOLOGY

DESIGN & TECHNOLOGY   MODERN FOREIGN LANGUAGE

PHYSICAL EDUCATION   CITIZENSHIP

plus

RELIGIOUS EDUCATION (statutory)

and *may* include

PERSONAL SOCIAL HEALTH EDUCATION:
(Careers, Sex Education, Drugs Education, Record of
Achievement/Progress File)

*NB: If schools do not have Personal Social Health Education,
then they must find alternative ways of delivering statutory
careers and sex education.*

together with a range of optional subjects

e.g. GEOGRAPHY – HISTORY – ART – MUSIC – PE

           GNVQ • Business
                   • Health & Social Care
                   • Travel &Tourism

or

ALTERNATIVE CURRICULUM provision

      e.g. link with • College
                   • Training Provider
                   • Work Experience

Figure 2.3 The secondary curriculum at Key Stage 4

The wider curriculum

Aspects of the wider curriculum are delivered in a variety of ways. All teachers are expected to promote spiritual, moral, social and cultural education, for example, through their lessons, but this aspect may also be made explicit through the statutory religious education and citizenship lessons as well as non-statutory personal, social and health education lessons. The pupils' personal and social development is further fostered through the pastoral curriculum, which may include taught PSHE lessons as well as tutorial sessions in secondary schools. In fact many secondary schools use the PSHE lessons to ensure that they cover the statutory requirements of sex education and careers education. An important contribution is also made by the school ethos, by relationships within the school, through school assemblies and extra-curricular activities.

It is easy to see from all of this that children in schools are under a constant pressure to perform. In light of this it is clear that a Learning Mentor has a huge role to play in the life of a school. They are expected to provide a complementary service to existing teachers and pastoral staff and provide services to young people and their families outside school. The question is, where do they fit into the structure?

Staffing structure

A Learning Mentor is employed by a school and should have a defined role based around the directive from the Excellence in Cities initiative, that of engaging those pupils who may be experiencing 'barriers to learning'. As part of a whole school staffing structure the mentor should discover where they are placed within the system and to whom they are accountable. There will be differences from school to school. All organisations have these differences but, irrespective of this, there should be a named person designated as their line manager. This person's role will be to both support and evaluate the work undertaken by the Learning Mentor. In some larger schools this may involve more than one person, where there may be a senior Learning Mentor plus assistant Learning Mentors.

For the purpose of the Learning Mentor, Figures 2.4 and 2.5 provide generic structures for imaginary primary and secondary schools. This gives an overview of the personnel employed and, in turn, those who may be available to support the Learning Mentor in performing their role. What is not included in the structures, however, is the vast number of adults who support the work of the school but are not directly employed by it. Many of these will become close work colleagues of the Learning Mentor. Additionally the Learning Mentor will receive further support from the LEA's Link Learning Mentor and Learning Mentor Networks.

Getting to know the school

In order to make total sense of the school organisation and curriculum, Learning Mentors should have an induction into the school that allows them to gain a picture

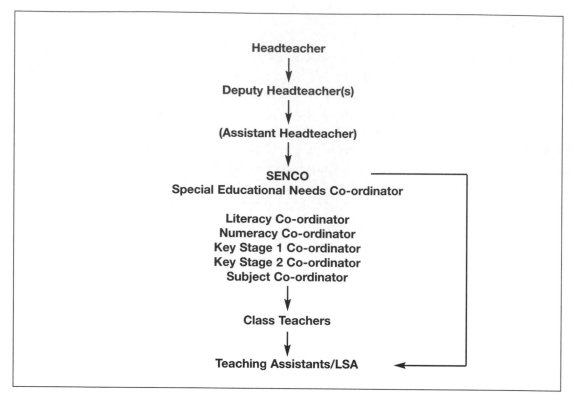

Figure 2.4 Primary school organisation

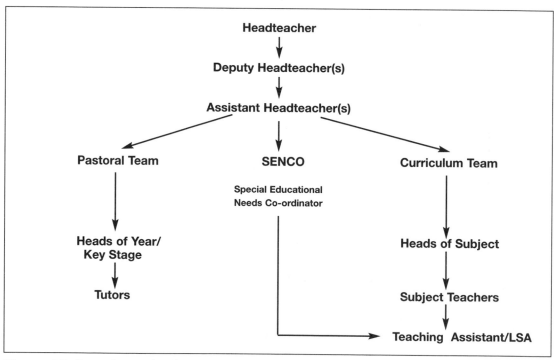

Figure. 2.5 Secondary school organisation

There may be other designated responsibilities within the school and there will also be a number of non-teaching staff employed by the school who will have designated line managers for their particular area of expertise.

Practical issues

- Map of the school
- Staff lists/lists of pupils
- School timetable
- Timings for the school day
- Calendar of activities for the term/year

Introduction/Meeting

- Office manager – administrative routines explained
- Senior Manager – roles and responsibilities outlined, decision-making processes explained
- Special Education Needs Co-ordinator – application of the Code of Practice and outline of assessment processes
- Pastoral manager (or Deputy Head in primary schools) – discussion of the role of heads of year and tutors in secondary schools/extended role of class teacher in primary schools. Socio-economic context of school and families explained
- Person responsible for cross phase transfer, whether it be infant/primary, primary/secondary or secondary/post-16, to outline processes and paperwork
- Education welfare officer/attendance officer/home–school liaison worker
- Non-teaching staff such as lunchtime supervisors for discussion about playground and break/lunchtime concerns
- Designated teachers for Child Protection and Looked After Children

Observation

- English and mathematics lessons
- Practical lessons such as art, PE, music
- Tutor/registration period
- Children at break time and lunchtime
- Extra-curricular activities
- Arrival at and departure from school
- Assemblies

School policies and practice

- School handbook
- Policies on
  - Child Protection
  - Special Needs
  - Behaviour, including rewards and sanctions
  - Equal Opportunities
  - Homework
  - Health and Safety
  - Home–school liaison
  - Confidentiality

School meetings

- Full Staff
- Pastoral
- Curriculum/Subject
- Parent

Figure 2.6 Checklist for Learning Mentor induction

of what goes on in the school on a day-to-day basis. Some aspects need to be dealt with as soon as the Learning Mentor starts at the school, others could be phased in at different times during the year. The needs of Learning Mentors are very diverse in this respect. While some Learning Mentors are ex-teachers, others come from a range of backgrounds and their previous experience of schools may only be that of themselves as a pupil. The purpose of the induction programme therefore would be to familiarise the Learning Mentors with the school and its community and should not be seen as anything more. Suggested elements that would provide for an introduction into a school are outlined in the 'Induction Programme Checklist' (Figure 2.6). Following on from this induction, a more complex training programme should be planned, focusing on issues pertinent to the Learning Mentors and their specific role (this will be discussed further in Chapter 9).

Although many schools may produce their own handbook and information packs for Learning Mentors that include much of the information outlined, there is an essential element to an induction programme that should not be ignored, and that is, it gives the Learning Mentor the opportunity to talk to people, observe the school at work and begin to feel a part of it. In addition to this, the school should also assign a member of the school staff who is responsible for dealing with the day-to-day practical support of the Learning Mentor, especially in terms of helping them to access information and find resources.

In respect of the working relationship between the school staff and the Learning Mentor, schools should consider a training session or handbook on the role of the Learning Mentor. This would serve to establish a whole school approach and perhaps prevent misunderstanding or conflict of interest from taking place.

Having looked at the school's organisation, set-up and provision, let us now move forward and focus more fully on the role of the Learning Mentor supporting the learning of pupils.

3 Barriers to learning

Being challenged with raising achievement, improving attendance and reducing exclusion is, by any stretch of the imagination, a daunting one. A pupil who has become disaffected and reluctant to engage in learning is by no means going to prove easy to re-motivate and may prove difficult to work with, so why on earth would anyone take it on? Simple – making a difference to a child's life, enabling them to move forward and progress and to see them succeed is one of the finest rewards that can be had. The question is – how do you do it? Well, in order to re-engage the child in learning the first step to take is to discover what may be causing the blockage!

Causes of barriers to learning

Whenever there is reluctance to learn, there is always, most definitely, a reason for it. The difficulty, however, is discovering what that reason might be.

There are many internal and external factors that impact upon a child, at any one time. Figure 3.1 demonstrates the use of a mind-mapping technique to develop thoughts about what may actually influence a child both in and out of school. It is a very simple exercise to go through and, by extending each 'branch' into further 'branches', it is relatively easy to gain 'the bigger picture' of the wide range of factors that can affect a school population. This could also be seen by a Learning Mentor as a useful working document; adding new branches as new 'situations' come to the forefront will provide a useful record of the range of work undertaken.

Now take a few moments to consider the example in Figure 3.1. Think about the wide variety of influences/situations that are listed here (you will undoubtedly think of more as you look at each set of branches – they are by no means finite) and consider their impact upon the child.

From this point we can perhaps begin to understand why some children find it difficult to cope with the demands placed upon them in school. It is, however, not good enough to just acknowledge the existence of such problems, we need to look further to discover how they might affect the child. Think! – How would you cope with some of those stresses and strains? How would you react? What would you do? Would you really be able to concentrate on your schoolwork? Whatever we do, however we do it, there is a need to realise that central to any form of response is the

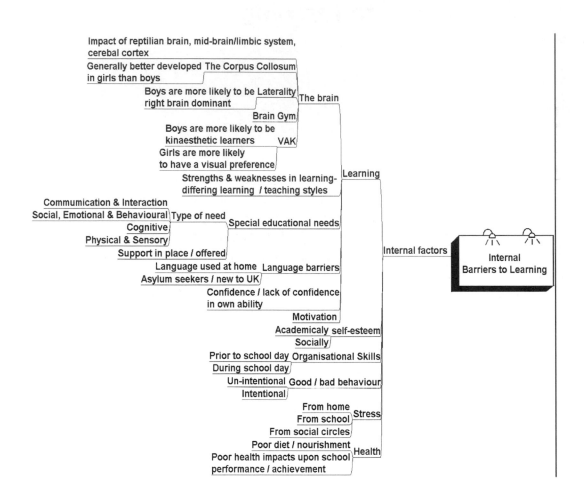

Figure 3.1 Factors affecting learning

External Barriers to Learning

External Factors

home

Are there any family pressures?
- Are there any financial pressures?
- What is the impact of a parent/ carer leaving suddenly?
- Is the child dealing with family bereavement?

Is it a learning environment?
- Do the parents / carers help, have the ability to help?
- Does the home provide a positive & condusive environment for homework?

What is the attitude to learning & achievement
- negative?
- positive?

Are there any social factors impacting upon the child?
- Is the child comfortable / frightened in their local environment?
- Is a neighbourly feud impacting upon school?
- Are there any negative influences in the local environment?
- Is there any influence from alcohol or drugs on the life of the child?

What are the relationships between siblings (if any)?

Does the child have responsibilities as a young carer?

Is there a general lack of aspiration in respect of education and schools
- Is it due impact of parent(s) own poor experiences of school?
- Is perception of unemployment lack of employment opportunity a factor
- Are there local social factors / influences that may impact upon the child / family

Is there a good relationship between school / home
- Do parents have open access to school
- Are there language / cultural barriers that are causing misunderstanding?

Bereavement

school

Access to curriculum
- Is the child able to understand & function in the classroom without additional help?
  - Is it a problem related to the child's academic ability / social functioning
  - Is it a problem due to poor curriculum planning / delivery by the teacher?
- Is the curriculum suited to the child
  - Is the child motivated to learn?
  - Does the curriculum meet the long-term needs of the child?
- P.E. Lessons
  - Are problems with uniform / kit causing confrontation with teacher
  - Does poor self-esteem in ability to perform cause stress and pressure on child
  - Self-conscious in undressing
- Do poor literacy & numeracy skills impact upon all learning

Social competences
- Is the child able to socialise with:
  - teachers?
  - support staff?
  - other pupils?
- Is the child able to take instruction / / direction / criticism / be challenged from:
  - teachers?
  - support staff?
  - other pupils?
- Is the child able to take care of themself in respect of health & hygeine?

Peer pressure / friends influence
- In the company of other children is the child:
  - passive?
  - dominant?
- Has bullying ever taken place:
  - against the child?
  - by the child against others?
- How does the child react around other children in:
  - the classroom
  - outside of the learning environment e.g. playground, dining room

processing that takes place within the brain. It is here that we are going to look towards discovering what happens when we are under pressure, when we feel stressed and in turn, how this might affect our actions.

In the last 15–20 years there have been major developments in the understanding of how the brain works. It has allowed a great deal of information to be shared regarding how we actually learn. We can discover by reading a whole range of books (see additional reading books) and associated research what happens inside the brain when movement and learning take place. More importantly for the Learning Mentor, we can discover the possible effects of some of the situations and influences outlined in Figure 3.1 on the brain and, in turn, how that affects the child in the learning situation.

The brain

Let us begin with a brief look at the brain. We are going to examine the basic functions of three identified areas as outlined in Figure 3.2.

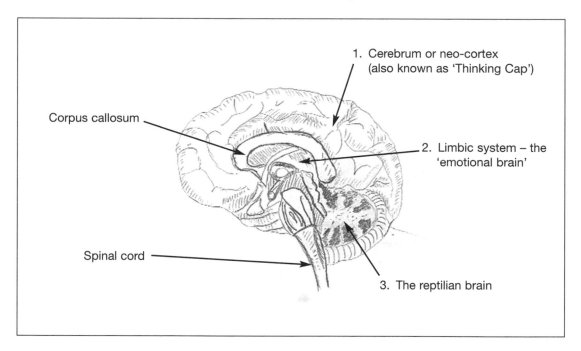

Figure 3.2 The brain

The three numbered areas of the diagram have a vital link to each other and in order to fully comprehend the way in which the brain responds we need to look at the role of each and how they interact. The first part we are going to look at is the cerebrum: it is here where all of the hard work takes place; this part of the brain is constantly 'busy'.

1 – The Thinking Cap (cerebrum/neo-cortex)

The name Thinking Cap is given to the cerebrum because it is here where we think, see, hear and imagine. It is here where our brain tries to make sense of the input it receives and searches to provide a response. The cerebrum has two hemispheres, left and right. These two hemispheres are connected by the corpus collosum (a bundle of nerves) which relays messages from one to the other. It enables the sharing of information and may be seen as being similar in its working to a computer search engine. The two hemispheres actually perform different functions, thus the need to 'search both sides'.

What the hemispheres have responsibility for ...	
LEFT HEMISPHERE	**RIGHT HEMISPHERE**
Language	Forms and patterns
Logic	Spatial awareness
Number	Images and pictures
Sequencing	Dimension
Analysis	Rhythm
Cause and effect	Musical appreciation
Time consciousness	Sport
Step-by-step processing	Imagination
Unrelated factual information	Whole picture processing
Phonetic reading/spelling	Whole word reading/spelling

We can perhaps begin to understand why this part of the brain is constantly busy, as it continually searches for responses, moving from one hemisphere to the other looking for responses to the input received. Have you ever heard someone say that their brain is tired? Well perhaps it is perfectly true! While this processing is in action, part 2 of the brain, the limbic system, is constantly influencing what is happening 'upstairs' in the Thinking Cap.

2 – 'Emotional Brain' – 'Middle Brain' (the limbic system)

The limbic system has several functions, but as we are taking a 'quick tour' of the brain and not an in-depth study the focus will be on the following:

- The filtering of information
- Positive and negative emotions
- Long-term memory

FILTERING INFORMATION

The reticular system filters information that is useful, needed and valued while at the same time it marginalises less useful information and ignores the useless. This helps us to work effectively and prevents overload. Imagine what it would be like if we didn't have this ability; we would be constantly barraged with a huge amount of input. As it is, we process that which is important.

POSITIVE AND NEGATIVE EMOTIONS

Emotional responses are controlled by the limbic system. Take a short time to consider each one of the following words:

Look at the six words in the boxes, one at a time – what are your first thoughts, what are you feelings as you look at each in turn?		
HOSPITAL	**?**	**SCHOOL BELL**
FIGHTING		**SWIMMING**
SUNSHINE		**FRIEND**

Whatever your reaction, you will most certainly have immediately recalled memories associated with each word. You will have perhaps visualised past memories, felt past emotions, remembered particular smells, maybe recalled particular incidents. The brain values these emotional responses more than the higher-order thinking skills because your emotional experiences help you to remember. This is a very important factor to be considered when engaging children in learning.

THE LONG-TERM MEMORY

This is simple! As it suggests, it is here where those emotional experiences, feelings and memories are kept.

It would seem then from the information gleaned, the limbic system is vital to the learning process and, if it is to be effective, account must be taken of the emotional experiences of the children. There is, however, one more area of the brain that we have to consider, and it is here that, when children are under stress, the greatest effect on learning takes place.

3. – The reptilian brain

The reptilian brain is the oldest part of our brain. During evolution the reptilian brain was the first part to develop. It was and is responsible for basic survival. When under stress or pressure this part of the brain takes control and the following takes place:

• Blood flows away from higher-order thinking areas and back down to the reptilian brain to support the survival response
• Chemicals are pumped into the bloodstream to make sure the body can respond quickly while under threat

- The heart rate increases
- The blood flow is focused towards the vital organs for survival
- Blood pressure goes up
- The muscles get ready to respond quickly

The result of all of this is that the rest of the brain effectively closes down. Any idea of a child learning in such a situation is futile. The effects of the above make it impossible. The brain will focus on the source/cause of the stress, and what is commonly known as the 'fight, freeze or flight' response will take place. The child will remain and argue/fight, or freeze and not respond, or they will run away from the situation. Even those who are able to control their emotions to some degree will still find it difficult to engage in learning.

Consider the following:

> **A child's mother is in hospital undergoing an operation. Her father thinks it is better to send her to school to keep her mind busy. The child goes to the first lesson where the teacher is introducing a new topic that is going to require a great deal of concentration and processing of information.**
>
> *Where is the child's mind focused – on the work or on mother?*

> **A child is in a lesson when one of the other children whispers that they are going to 'get them' later that morning. The child is a quiet shy type who does not like arguments or fighting.**
>
> *Is this child's mind going to remain on task for the rest of the lesson or is it going to focus on the impending argument/fight?*

> **A child who has a learning difficulty experiences difficulty in reading. As the children go into the classroom, the teacher tells them that during the lesson they are going to be reading Harry Potter, in turn, around the class.**
>
> *Is the child following the story as others read or dwelling on the fact that their turn to read is getting ever closer?*

> ***Now think of a situation where you have been under pressure in a learning situation. What do you remember the most – the situation or what you were learning at the time?***

Having spent time considering the range of pressures and stresses that children may face and in turn how their reaction to these can affect learning, we can perhaps now have a wider perception of why such children may have problems with, for example:

- Attendance/extended absence
- Bullying
- Low self-esteem

- Emotional difficulties
- Motivation
- Behaviour
- Achievement

If we are to help them to overcome these we need to look at how we might support them and enable them to re-engage in learning.

Removing the barriers

In order to do this the learning mentor should have some mechanism to establish what the child's difficulties are and to ascertain the type of action/support to be given/accessed. This should be done (through discussion with the child) at the action planning stage. However, the method of working this out is not the important factor here (there are a variety of strategies in use by Learning Mentors), it is that the action taken is appropriate.

Momentarily return to Figure 3.1 and take time once again to look through the issues listed. If the Learning Mentor is able to change the child's circumstances and, in turn, take away some or all of the pressure, this should be the first consideration. For example, if a child has a conflict with a teacher, is it possible to arrange for them to move groups? If homework is a problem can they have time in school with adult support to complete it? Where the pressure cannot be alleviated by such actions then we must find ways of helping the child to deal with the pressure or, as we have seen, the reptilian brain may well take control.

The case studies which follow indicate some ways in which Learning Mentors have worked to overcome pressures that have impacted on school performance. Names and contexts have been adapted in order to preserve anonymity. As you read through them, consider how you would have responded. The special relationship between the Learning Mentor and the pupil, the social context of the school and its environment makes it likely that no two people will respond in the same way.

Bereavement

I had been working with Sarah (aged 13) for only a few weeks. She had been referred to me because she had become rather withdrawn and her attendance was deteriorating. Sarah didn't speak much about her family, and certainly didn't want me to visit her at home when she was away. I had spoken to her mother on the telephone at the start of the mentoring process.

When Sarah had been away for a week, and no-one seemed to know why, I rang the home and was shocked to be told that Sarah's mother had died earlier in the week. The funeral was taking place on the next day, but her father didn't know when Sarah would be back at school.

Few people, unless they are professional bereavement counsellors, feel totally at ease talking to people who have recently been bereaved but, with research indicating that each year about 14,500 children in England and Wales are bereaved of a parent, it is likely to be something with which the Learning Mentor is going to have to cope. In Sarah's case, the death of her mother was not unexpected to the family as she had been suffering from lung cancer for many years. Sarah had been gradually taking on her mother's role with respect to her two younger brothers, and her father had been becoming more dependent on her to help with cooking and cleaning around the house. Sarah had chosen not to share her situation with the school. She could only cope if she was left to deal with the situation in her own way, and was very concerned about what would happen now that the school knew.

Although Sarah was not at first happy about intervention by the Learning Mentor, it was important that someone at school contacted the family after the bereavement to show concern and offer help, but it also lets the pupil know that the school is now aware of their changed circumstances. If children have been happy at school, it is recommended that they return to school as soon as possible as the familiar routines of a school can be very comforting, supportive and safe. A major factor that influences the outcome of grieving is the support a child receives from adults and other young people and so the Learning Mentor should have strategies in place for when a bereaved child returns. Loss typically has a profound effect on the learning and behaviour of a child, and so the school needs to be alert to any changes. Equally, there is a need to be wary of a child who appears to be quietly coping with their grief as they may be exhibiting signs of depression.

In *Death and Bereavement* (NAPCE 1997), guidance is offered about what the school can do when a child is bereaved, and this includes:

- Take cues from their behaviour about how they feel
- All children react differently – aggressiveness, anger, guilt, fear, regression, withdrawal are all signs of grief – take this into account
- Grieving affects concentration and attainments – help children with this
- Children may deny grief and grieving may be delayed – this needs to be recognised
- Bereaved children need to re-establish a self-identity
- If a pupil seeks you out be available and listen with your ears, eyes and heart
- Be ready for questions and be open and honest with feelings
- Ensure that teachers and pupils know about the bereavement and know how to help
- Provide a quiet place
- Help the pupil's friends to be helpful
- Ensure good contact with the family and don't underestimate how you can help through such an open and honest approach
- Offer practical help

The Learning Mentor also needs to be alert to separation anxiety whereby the child becomes fearful of leaving home in case something else happens in their absence.
In Sarah's case, the Learning Mentor was able to effect a return to school although it did take a few weeks. Allowances were made for a late arrival in the mornings as she had to ensure that her brothers were organised to go to school. Help was also given with regard to homework as Sarah's domestic responsibilities sometimes made it

unreasonable for her to have to complete homework after cooking meals, and sorting out her brothers' problems. The Learning Mentor arranged a quiet place where she could work at lunchtimes if she chose to do so, but this had the negative effect of reducing time for social contact with the few friends that she had. Underachievement seems inevitable, but with the additional help of a Personal Adviser, the mentor continues to monitor Sarah's progress.

More commonly the Learning Mentor may have to find ways of offering comfort to a youngster whose pet has died. The death of a family pet can render a child inconsolable, and it may be the first time that a child has had to come to terms with the finality of death. In such situations parents often choose to send their child to school 'to take their mind off' the bereavement and thus there is an expectation that the school will find ways of helping the child to cope.

Bullying

The class teacher became concerned when just before playtime Jamie (aged 8) said he felt sick and didn't want to go outside. She telephoned his mother, who agreed to come and collect him and take him home. He returned the next day and was initially fine but again, as playtime approached he became clingy and asked the Teaching Assistant if he could stay with her at playtime. Rather than agree to his again staying inside, the Teaching Assistant went outside with him at playtime. She observed a group of boys watching him as they ran to the far end of the playground to play football. The next day, Jamie stayed away. He told his mother that he had got stomach ache.

Clearly there was a problem at school and the Learning Mentor was asked to spend time with Jamie to try to ascertain what was wrong. Other boys in the class were calling him names in the playground and making comments about his trainers. They did not allow him to play football with them and so at playtime he just had to stand around by himself. Jamie did not want to come to school, and certainly couldn't concentrate on his work because he was constantly worried about what would happen when he went outside.

The first thing that the Learning Mentor wanted to do was to get to know Jamie and gain his trust. He was still reluctant to attend school and so the Learning Mentor invited his mother to bring him in to meet her. Once the initial contact had been made, the Learning Mentor arranged to meet Jamie the next morning on his arrival in school. They had a chat, and the mentor told Jamie to come and spend his playtime with her. This set a pattern for the first week. By the end of the week, Jamie was willingly talking with the Learning Mentor, but was still not willing to go outside at playtime. During the second week, Jamie joined a small group that the mentor met with weekly to build self-esteem. He also had time alone with the mentor, during which they planned his return to the playground and discussed coping strategies. While the Learning Mentor was working with Jamie, the class teacher was working with the rest of the class. She had decided to adopt a combination of the 'no blame' approach and circle time to explore issues around the nature of bullying with the whole class. During circle time discussions with the class in which the bully group was included, the teacher tried to establish a climate of peer support for pupils who could be victims of bullying. Jamie was present for some of the sessions. During the third week Jamie, accompanied by the Learning Mentor, went into the playground. He was ignored by the boys with whom he used to play football, but one of the boys from the 'building self-esteem' group came up to talk with them.

Bullying is a major contributor to the underachievement of some pupils and is also a growth area in the field of litigation. There are many definitions, but in general it involves any behaviour which is deliberately intended to hurt, threaten or frighten another person, and usually involves an imbalance or abuse of power. It can involve a range of behaviours which include:

- physically aggressive – hitting, kicking, taking or damaging belongings;
- verbal – name-calling, nasty teasing or spreading rumours;
- indirect – deliberately leaving someone out or ignoring someone.

Jamie was victim of both verbal and indirect bullying from boys who gained power through being part of a group. In the bullying relationship, they initially stuck together although through the work the class teacher undertook, the rest of the class ignored them and showed their support for Jamie. Through support from the Learning Mentor, Jamie learnt strategies to better cope with the situation and gained new friends through membership of the mentor's 'self-esteem' group. Jamie gradually regained confidence and felt able to go outside at playtimes, but he always knew that should problems re-emerge, he could get support from the Learning Mentor.

Tackling bullying has to be a whole school issue and the Learning Mentor stands a better chance of an effective intervention if there is a climate within the school that clearly emphasises that bullying will not be tolerated. This is particularly important because much bullying is subtle and difficult to detect by adults, while being very distressing to the child. Figure 3.3 shows some comments made by bullies and their victims, and has been used to highlight some of these issues both with bullies and their victims.

Many Learning Mentors have engaged in assertiveness training sessions with small groups of children who have been victims of bullies, and these tend to follow the pattern of similar courses outlined in *Bullying: Don't Suffer in Silence* (DfE 1994). The younger the pupils, the shorter the sessions should be and the smaller the group. The assertiveness groups run once a week for between six and eight weeks and research undertaken on such work in primary schools indicates that the optimum time for pupils in years 4 and 5 was twenty minutes with a maximum of six to eight pupils. In the sessions, the pupils were taught how to

- make assertive statements
- resist manipulation and threats
- respond to name-calling
- leave a bullying situation
- escape safely from physical restraint
- enlist the support of bystanders
- boost their own self-esteem
- remain calm in stressful situations.

Figure 3.3 Bullying and the victim

Of course bullies also have need of help, and it is possible that the Learning Mentor will be asked to help the bully reflect on his/her behaviour. Invariably bullies, while outwardly appearing tough, suffer from low self-esteem and bring with them a whole raft of problems.

Extended Absence

Carl, aged 11, did not go to school. He was on roll in year 7 at St George's High School but had never attended. Carl had visited the school when he was in year 6 at Hill Heath Junior School and St George's had invited him and his parents to several meetings but they had never responded. Carl liked school and had attended regularly at Hill Heath, but his parents had never sent him to the secondary school. As a result Carl was bored and started mixing with older boys on the housing estate where he lived. He soon came to the attention of the police, who duly contacted St George's School for further information about him.

Although the Education Welfare Officer at St George's School had made a few visits to Carl's home, she had never obtained any response. She had left a letter asking the parents to contact her at the school. The police request for information made Carl a priority case at the school, and so the Learning Mentor was asked to work with the EWO to investigate the current situation.

The Learning Mentor and EWO decided first to make a visit to Carl's primary school to find out more about him and his family. Carl had enjoyed school when he was younger and had attended regularly. The family had been reasonably supportive, and his mother had attended all the parents' meetings. They lived close to the school. The Learning Mentor and Education Officer decided to make yet another visit to Carl's home. Previous visits had been made during the daytime so they decided on an evening meeting. They did attempt to telephone beforehand but got no response and decided to go anyway. When they arrived at the home, the mother was in but Carl was not. She expressed surprise that Carl had not been attending school. She left home at 6.30 a.m. and assumed that he got himself up and went to school. She did not recollect receiving any letters about his absence from school, and it was assumed that Carl was intercepting the post. She didn't really know where Carl's new school was but stated that now he was in the secondary school he had to be responsible for himself. The meeting was fairly amicable, but nothing could be resolved without Carl so a further appointment was made for the next evening when Carl's mother would make sure that he was at home.

At the next meeting Carl agreed that he had not attended school and gave two reasons. Firstly he did not have any money for the bus fare or for his dinners, and secondly, he did not have any friends at the new school so he was worried about going there himself. His mother did not realise that Carl needed money. He used to walk to his junior school, and he had free dinners. The Learning Mentor and Education Welfare Officer agreed a plan of action. The EWO would help to sort out Carl's school uniform and arrange for him to have free dinners. The Learning Mentor would collect Carl and his mother from their home and take them to the new school to meet the Head of Year and some of the pupils. A phased entry to the school was then agreed.

For the first week Carl would attend for mornings only and the Learning Mentor would make sure that he knew which bus he needed to catch in order to get to the school in time. This plan was put into effect and was mainly successful. Although Carl managed to get to school every day, he had missed so much work that he needed a considerable amount of support in lessons. He also had problems mixing with the other pupils, but the Learning Mentor included him in a small group session about self-esteem where he got to know a small number of other pupils. Progress is slowly being made, but all concerned know that it would not take much for Carl to stop attending and so his attendance is being carefully monitored.

This is a fairly extreme example, but many children do not attend school willingly and can easily be put off attending. The form tutor or class teacher is usually the first person that the pupil meets each day, and being made to feel welcome can make all the difference. If the pupils feel confident and positive at the start of the day, this feeling may well be sustained throughout the day and it is likely that they will want to attend. Pupils also want to feel that they are missed and many schools have a system of first-day calling which involves someone in the school contacting home on the first day of absence to find out reasons for non-attendance. While there are reasons to do with the journey to school, or family issues, which make regular attendance difficult for pupils, and will be considered elsewhere, the Learning Mentor needs to be alert to 'The School Effect'(Table 3.1).

Emotional problems

Sanjeev, year 7, was referred to me by his head of year. He was a bright pupil who was seriously underachieving and was always out of lessons, either refusing to go in, or having been sent out. He seemed to be getting into confrontational situations with teachers. There had been a dramatic change in his attitude and the head of year suspected that there had been an incident in Sanjeev's life which had provoked the decline in his work and behaviour.

I spoke with Sanjeev on two occasions, and at the second meeting he started to tell me about an incident which had happened about six weeks earlier. While Sanjeev and his younger brother were alone in their home someone broke in, assaulted the two boys and stole some items. Both lads were injured and had to go to hospital, but Sanjeev's greatest concern was his feeling of guilt that he couldn't either protect his brother or stop the burglary from taking place. There has been a dramatic breakdown in family relationships since the incident. Sanjeev has become very aggressive and throws household items around the house. His younger brother has become frightened of him.

As the Learning Mentor got to know Sanjeev better he realised that he needed professional help. He should have been seen by Victim Support soon after the incident, but they had cancelled the appointment and not made another one. The Learning Mentor, having got permission from the family, contacted Victim Support and Sanjeev had one appointment with a counsellor. Since the mentor's involvement, there had been a slight improvement in his behaviour and attitude, but he was still feeling very angry. The Learning Mentor telephoned the local Child and Adolescent Mental Health Services (CAMHS), who were very positive, but he was placed on a five-month-long waiting list. Sanjeev started to have time off school for

Table 3.1 The School Effect: some factors which contribute to pupil absence

Issues	Good practice by Learning Mentor
Teachers	
• sarcastic/insensitive • shout a lot • can't/don't control the class • unfair • unapproachable • too many supply teachers	The Learning Mentor needs to discuss these concerns with the line manager, who will be better placed to investigate the reality of the situation. In the meantime, the mentor should continue to encourage the pupil to attend and if necessary temporarily withdraw the pupil from a lesson that may be causing undue distress. This can of course only be a short-term solution. Arrange for the pupil to move to a different class.
Pupils	
• bullying • lack of friends • sexual harassment • racial harassment	The school should have policies in place to outline appropriate action and the mentor should follow such guidance. Establish peer mentoring/buddy systems. Promote self-esteem Take opportunities to celebrate diversity.
Routines	
• have not got correct uniform • no PE kit • no materials for practical lessons • no money for school visit • no note to explain absence	Ensure families have access to all entitlements. Have an awareness of home circumstances. Act as advocate on behalf of the child.
Academic performance	
• inappropriate curriculum • inappropriate teaching methods • poor basic skills • problems with homework and coursework deadlines • stress – linked to tests and examinations • fear of failure	Consider alternative curriculum provision. Discuss preferred learning styles with pupils. Talk to line manager about teaching strategies. Undertake lesson observation. Study support/homework clubs. Plan for reintegration following absence. Stress management/time management. Involve pupils in target-setting.
The environment	
• poor toilet facilities • lack of secure place to keep belongings • little to do in the playground • forced outside at breaks/lunchtimes • poor decorative state	Try to involve pupils in spending decisions that affect their environment. Work with lunchtime supervisors – organise lunchtime activities. Good quality displays, including pupils' own work.

a range of not very convincing medical reasons. The Learning Mentor called an in-school conference about Sanjeev and it was generally felt that he could be clinically depressed. As a result of the meeting, the Learning Mentor took Sanjeev, with his mother to a local psychiatric practice for a 'drop-in' session. As a result of this intervention, the psychiatrist contacted CAMHS and Sanjeev's case was made a priority. He was seen within two weeks.

A report from the Mental Health Foundation (1999) claims that one in five children and teenagers suffer from mental health problems. It is estimated that one in ten have problems sufficiently severe to require professional help, more than 8 per cent have difficulty getting on with their everyday lives and 12 per cent have anxiety disorders. Depression also affects young people. Graham and Hughes (1995) estimated that about 2 per cent of children under the age of 12 are sufficiently depressed as to need the help of a child psychologist, whereas about 5 per cent at this age show signs of significant distress. The rate goes up with age and so about 5 per cent of teenagers may be seriously depressed and at least twice that number show significant distress. In areas with high rates of broken homes, poor community support and raised neighbourhood crime rates the level of depression may be considerably higher.

Although the Learning Mentor can work effectively with pupils who have emotional and psychological problems, for long-term effectiveness support from specialists will be needed. It is also important that the Learning Mentor works with the family, as their support will be vital. As demonstrated in the case study, referral to specialists can take a long time and the Learning Mentor should work with the appropriate person in the school such as the SENCO or school nurse to ensure that correct referral channels are used. This is an area where Learning Mentors need to know their limits and hand the matter over to the professionals and ensure that the pupil receives best possible care from the appropriate agency.

Dealing with Anger

Charlie's year 5 teacher was very concerned because Charlie was progressively becoming aggressive in his response to other pupils when he couldn't get his own way. She referred him to me and asked if I could talk to him as she felt that in addition to the disruption it was causing, it was also making Charlie very unhappy.

I decided to meet with Charlie's mother before talking to him as I wanted to gain a full picture of his behaviour both in and out of school. Charlie's mother told me that he had from time to time had temper tantrums which she felt had been usual for a small child and just a part of growing up, but he had not always been so aggressive. She was becoming more concerned because Charlie seemed to be getting involved in more fights at home while playing with friends.

I met with Charlie for two weeks and chatted informally about school and his general interests. At the point where I felt confident that our relationship was strong enough, I asked Charlie if he felt that there was a reason why he was getting into more trouble. Charlie talked about other children annoying him and the feelings of anger that were inside of him when he thought other children were being unfair. He said he couldn't help it when he lost his temper because he felt that he was 'on fire' inside and the only way he could get rid of that feeling was by arguing and fighting. He said that he felt very upset afterwards and sorry that he had upset other people and that he felt he was not liked very much by the other children in his class.

I talked to Charlie about his anger and asked if he would like to work with me to look at ways of helping him to deal with the 'fire' that was upsetting him and to help him to feel better about himself.

The Learning Mentor organised through an outside agency access to anger management sessions with a support teacher who had been trained to deal with such issues. Charlie was introduced to the teacher by his mentor and they chatted together informally during the first session to allow Charlie to relax and gain confidence in his new 'helper'. It was agreed that the three of them should work together as a team.

Charlie began to use a range of strategies for dealing with his anger that he had discussed at the weekly meeting with the support teacher and his mentor. He would record in a special diary each time he had become angry and say what had made him angry. This then formed part of his next session where each time the three would talk about ways in which he could deal with the anger to prevent him from losing his temper with others. This included Charlie having a 'time out' card that could be shown to the teacher at a point when he felt he was about to lose control. He would be excused from the class so that he could find the Learning Mentor who would talk to him and allow him time to calm down before taking him back to rejoin his class. At this point the mentor would stay in the classroom until confident that Charlie and the class were once again settled with each other.

As things improved, at one of his weekly meetings Charlie said that he was feeling much better and getting in 'a lot less trouble' because of the help he was getting but he was sad that some of the children in his class didn't talk much to him anymore. He said it was because he had been horrible to them before. Charlie was ready to build bridges but he didn't know how. It was decided to organise circle time activities in small groups with a focus on sharing feelings so that Charlie could, in a structured setting, let the children know and understand how difficult it sometimes was for him. It would also allow Charlie to understand more fully the distress he sometimes caused to others. Through the session it was hoped to build up shared strategies of support for the whole group. The sessions worked very well and at the end of the focused intervention both Charlie and the class felt they had become much closer to understanding how to help each other.

There are many children in schools who feel the way that Charlie feels. He is struggling to deal with his anger. He does not have the self-control required to deal with the pressures both within the classroom and beyond. There is a definite need for structured support. The Learning Mentor dealt with the situation practically and with sensitivity. Children such as Charlie will not be able to function without some form of intervention, and we would suggest that anger management has to be the first port of call. Imagine Charlie at the age of 14 without any intervention having taken place!

Accessing anger management services can be done through external agencies. They may provide support workers, or mentors may even consider undergoing training themselves so that they are able to provide support to the children without external intervention. There will be additional information on accessing such support in Chapter 9, which looks at professional development and training.

The PE lesson

I was asked to work with Zoe because she had been spasmodically truanting from school for several weeks.

During the first meeting she was reluctant to talk but, after gaining her trust, she started to talk about her weight problem. We talked about how she felt and what her relationships with the other children were like. It was during this time that she admitted that she had been truanting from school on the days she couldn't persuade her mother to write excuse notes for the PE lesson. She said she was embarrassed about her body and hated getting undressed in front of the other girls.

This is not an unusual situation. There may be a variety of reasons why children do not want to go to their PE lesson; for example:

- Can't afford 'trendy' training shoes
- Haven't got the correct PE uniform
- Do not like taking off their clothes in front of other children
- Hate having to take a shower
- Are not good at sport
- Hate being the last one every time to be chosen for a team

Whatever the reason, it is obvious that these types of situation may well cause distress to a child, and in order to avoid any one of them, they may use a number of avoidance tactics, such as:

- Feigning illness and asking for notes from their parent/carer
- Feigning illness in school
- Forging notes
- Truanting the PE lesson/truanting whole day
- Forgetting PE kit

Solving the problem is not going to be an easy task and the Learning Mentor will need to be both sympathetic to the child's needs while at the same time being aware of the requirements of the law – that all children, unless for a bona fide medical reason, must take part in physical education lessons. For this reason, the PE teacher is likely to be very reluctant, even stubborn at times, in making allowances. It is here, therefore, that a conflict of interest may occur. The Learning Mentor is faced with the problem of supporting the child while at the same time supporting the PE teacher. This would definitely seem to be a 'no win' situation, but the Learning Mentor should consider that the interest of the child must be paramount at all times. The difficulty should be dealt with by looking at a range of strategies that alleviate the immediate stress while working towards longer-term solutions; for example:

- Arrange mentor meetings during PE lesson
- Restricted PE timetable
- Discussion with parent/carer
- Discuss problem with PE staff in relation to changing facilities

LONG-TERM

- Meeting with school nurse to deal with weight problem
- Work on developing self-esteem
- Join nurture group/circle time activity with girls from PE group to build up relationships/friendships
- Joint work with PE staff to develop support programme for Sarah to promote her physical ability rather than emphasise her weight

Taking part in PE lessons may be an area of conflict for a number of children who tolerate the situation and do not access the support of the Learning Mentor. Consideration should therefore be given to acceptable and workable solutions being shared within the school as they may well prevent difficulties for other pupils in the future. Zoe's mentor worked with the PE staff, school nurse and her mother to develop an approach that ensured Zoe felt supported and understood by all. The PE staff discussed a range of physical activities that would support the diet provided by the school nurse. Her mother in turn ensured her dietary requirements were met at home, while her mentor continued to meet with Zoe and involved her in circle time activities to develop her self-esteem. Zoe's progress was mapped by herself and the mentor during one-to-one sessions and, over a period of time, her weight and fitness improved, allowing her to take part in general PE activities with more confidence and feeling of self-worth.

After taking time to consider the case studies it is apparent that there are many varied situations that occur within schools with a wide range of possible interventions/solutions. In some cases, where further action may be required, this could involve:

- anger management
- relaxation techniques
- counselling
- family therapy
- access to financial help
- medical advice on, for example, eating disorders; smoking

The Learning Mentor must be aware that these types of intervention are specialised and they should look towards professional support to deliver associated programmes or embark on training to enable them to do so themselves.

Finally, if support is to be successful, irrespective of the type, there is a need for a trust and good working relationship between the mentor, the child and, where possible, the parents. It is from here we are now going to move forward to see how this may be achieved ...

4 Working with pupils and families

Working with pupils and their families is at the heart of the role of the Learning Mentor. By providing direct help in schools and access to a wider support network (if needed) the Learning Mentor can most certainly make a difference to the young person's chance of being successful. Spending time with individuals helping them to first identify their problems, then to accept them and finally to find ways of resolving them is the major contribution that a Learning Mentor can make.

The core work of the Learning Mentor involves raising attainment and achievement, improving attendance and helping the child to participate effectively in all that the school offers. In order to achieve this, the Learning Mentor needs to help the pupil with aspects such as:

- improving personal and social skills
- raising confidence and self-esteem
- increasing competence in basic skills
- improving organisational skills, including time management
- increasing motivation and the will to succeed
- improving relationships with peers and family
- increasing aspiration regarding post-16 options

In order to effect such improvements a variety of strategies will need to be adopted as each pupil's needs will be unique. Learning Mentors commonly work with a case load of between 10 and 15 pupils at any one time, but the degree of support given will range from in-depth support to keeping a watching brief. There will be those pupils requiring one-to-one individual support, while others may be better served being part of a small group. In addition to this, the Learning Mentor may also need to have time available for lesson observation, liaison with external agencies and home visits if appropriate. In view of all of this, it is apparent that Learning Mentors will need to be skilful time managers.

Explaining mentoring to pupils and parents

The Learning Mentor–pupil relationship can only be successful if the pupil is a willing participant in the process. In order for this to happen, the role of the mentor must be very carefully explained both to the pupil and to the parents, who are important partners in the learning process. This must be done sensitively to prevent the possibility of the pupil feeling stigmatised. The criteria for referral will vary from school to school, but in all cases they need to be fair and transparent to all.

Many schools produce leaflets for the pupils that explain the main principles of mentoring. Sample contents include

What do Learning Mentors do?
Who are the Learning Mentors?
What kind of problems can they help with?
How can a Learning Mentor help?
How often do pupils see their mentor?
How do people get chosen to have a Learning Mentor?

Regular newsletters can be useful in keeping parents, teachers and pupils informed about the work of the mentors and in helping them to maintain a high profile in the school (see Figure 4.1).

Ground rules

The Learning Mentor has an inherent advantage when working with children in that they are neither teachers nor parents. This does, however, bring with it a danger that the youngsters may misunderstand the role and overstep the professional boundary between mentor and pupil. It is important, therefore, that ground rules are established from the outset in order to protect both parties. These should focus around:

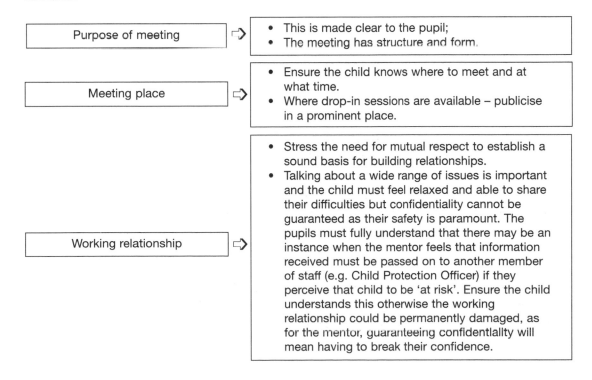

| Purpose of meeting | ⇨ | • This is made clear to the pupil;
 • The meeting has structure and form. |

| Meeting place | ⇨ | • Ensure the child knows where to meet and at what time.
 • Where drop-in sessions are available – publicise in a prominent place. |

| Working relationship | ⇨ | • Stress the need for mutual respect to establish a sound basis for building relationships.
 • Talking about a wide range of issues is important and the child must feel relaxed and able to share their difficulties but confidentiality cannot be guaranteed as their safety is paramount. The pupils must fully understand that there may be an instance when the mentor feels that information received must be passed on to another member of staff (e.g. Child Protection Officer) if they perceive that child to be 'at risk'. Ensure the child understands this otherwise the working relationship could be permanently damaged, as for the mentor, guaranteeing confidentiality will mean having to break their confidence. |

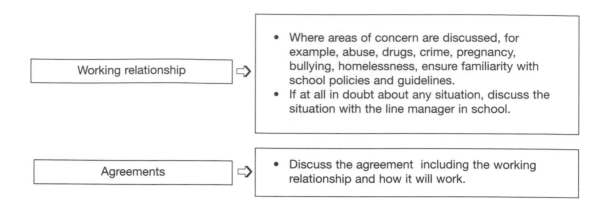

Working relationship	⇨	• Where areas of concern are discussed, for example, abuse, drugs, crime, pregnancy, bullying, homelessness, ensure familiarity with school policies and guidelines. • If at all in doubt about any situation, discuss the situation with the line manager in school.

Agreements	⇨	• Discuss the agreement including the working relationship and how it will work.

Appropriate location for meeting

This is a very important consideration if the Learning Mentor is to be able to effect a good working relationship with the child. One-to-one discussions can only be successful in private, calm and undisturbed settings. Factors that hinder such discussions include those external to the conversation, and this will most certainly be exacerbated by the use of an inappropriate environment. Schools are busy places and can be extremely noisy – not necessarily the noise of an unruly class, but those sounds that are routinely heard in any large institution, and so it is important that the location for any discussion is carefully selected. When choosing the working environment consideration of the following may help:

- Offices are ideal, but they should be in the main part of the school and obviously not, for example, next to the Music Room. One Learning Mentor who has an office next to the main school reception finds the location ideal. She is at the hub of activity, has quick access to the school office, and most importantly parents who come to visit her do not have to walk great distances through the school to meet her.
- Many Learning Mentors are based in the Learning Support Unit, or in the Special Needs Department, whereas others are adjacent to the pastoral area or the school library. In these areas access to internal and external support are often readily available; however, it is important to consider the point of view of the pupil, as the location of the Learning Mentor's office certainly gives a message about the nature of the service they are being offered.
- If one-to-one interviews are likely to be taking place, then the room should have a window (for child protection purposes) and the furniture should be arranged so that the viewing of both parties from outside is possible.
- While it is important that the room has a telephone to allow the Learning Mentor to maintain links with other parts of the school, families and support services, it should be possible for incoming calls to be diverted while an interview is taking place.
- A polite sign on the door of the meeting place should indicate that the Learning Mentor is not available for the duration of the interview so that interruptions are kept to a minimum. Interruptions will cause both parties to lose concentration but

Learning Mentor News

What do we do ?

By now, I am sure that many of you know a lot about us and our work, but for those of you who don't, let me explain. Learning mentors work in the school with individual pupils or small groups to help them overcome barriers to learning. This means, for example, that if a pupil has a problem and they are so worried about it that they cannot concentrate on their work, we can talk to them and help them solve their problem. It may be something simple like they don't understand their work because they have been ill and missed work. They can be given help and time to catch up. Other problems may be more complicated and need a longer time to sort out. Last week we started to help Steve who had been bullied for a few weeks but had finally been brave enough to tell someone about it. We shall be working with him for a few weeks until we are sure that he feels safe again in school. Farida and Shakie asked us to help them try to be more punctual so for two weeks they came to see us when they arrived in school and we signed a card for them to show their time of arrival. The main problems was that although Farida left home in time to get to school early, she called for Shakie who was never ready. When we heard that, we decided that Shakie needed her own alarm clock so helped her to buy one.

Teachers often ask us to help children who lack confidence or are not doing as well with their work as they should be.

We talk to them and try to find out what we can do to help. These are just a few of the things we do—if you want to know more, come and talk to us.

(children's names have been changed)

During half term we hope to arrange a visit to Moel Famau for our year 7 and 8 children (this is a mountain in Wales!) This will be good fun, but you do have to be fit to join in. More details will be put up on our notice board next week.

We shall also have one day in school where anyone who wants to spend some time catching up with work, or using the computers or books in the library can do so.

Attendance matters – a word to parents !

Children need to come to school regularly if they are going to learn and do well. Parents should only let their child stay away from school if they are too ill to attend. We often visit homes of children whose attendance is starting to worry us and really enjoy meeting and getting to know families. We would like to remind all parents, though, that if the school is ever closed to the pupils, say for a training day, you will always have a letter from the school telling you about it. Also, please do not let your child stay up half the night watching the television—they are often late and are fit for nothing when they come to school.

Who are we ?
Liz Evans

Jas Kaur

Kevin Williams

Learning mentors

Come and join us at
- Breakfast club
- Homework club
- Netball
- Football
- Dance club
- :

Have a nice day!

Figure 4.1 Newsletter

also may make a vulnerable pupil feel that s/he is encroaching on the time of the mentor.

- The room should be made comfortable, and have some pupil information and displays on the wall to personalise it.
- Secure storage facilities should also be available, e.g. for confidential pupil files.

Speaking and listening

Even when a suitable location for a conversation has been established, there are several other factors that can reduce the likelihood of effective listening taking place, and these are summarised in Figure 4.2.

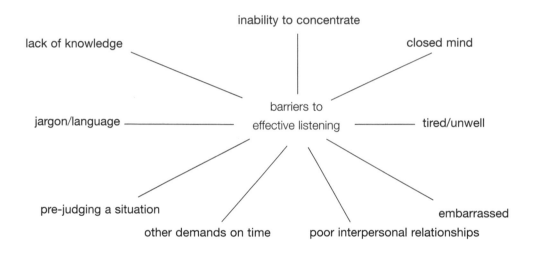

Figure 4.2 Barriers to effective listening

If the Learning Mentor wishes to help the pupils and fully gain their confidence, effective communication is essential. For many, the talking is easy whereas the art of effective listening has to be learnt. Children very quickly detect when they are not being listened to. Not only do inappropriate answers give an indication that the adult is not listening but, for example, yawning, looking at a watch, glancing out of the window will quickly be interpreted as boredom or lack of interest by the pupil who may well have used similar tactics. Interrupting the pupil by cutting in or finishing off sentences for them also suggests lack of interest. Similarly, the Learning Mentor must 'switch off' from all other concerns for the duration of the interview otherwise preoccupation with other matters will make effective listening impossible.

Good listening involves hearing, registering and understanding what is being said and planning an appropriate response. People are often surprised to discover how little of what they say is heard. The table below indicates the relative importance of the different elements of a conversation.

Verbal – what is said	7%
Tone of voice	38%
Visual – gestures/appearance	55%

It is important therefore that Learning Mentors are conscious of any unintended messages being given by their body language, facial expression and tone of voice. All too often youngsters, after a conversation with an adult, tell their friends 'I could tell s/he wasn't listening to what I was saying.' This is rarely the case, but it takes little to damage what may already be a tenuous relationship. Active listening can be conveyed through adopting appropriate posture, eye contact and making suitable responses, for example:

Posture – Have a relaxed posture and lean forward slightly to convey interest. Sitting defensively with folded arms and crossed legs can be off-putting. Never sit behind a desk but sit alongside the pupil or at an angle, but make sure that there is a comfortable distance between mentor and pupil.

Eye contact – Intermittent eye contact shows listening, but constant eye contact can be too intense. There is also a need to be aware of cultural issues, in that, for example, for some people not making eye contact may be a sign of respect.

Responses – Mentors must learn to be at ease with silence. Silence gives both parties time to reflect and formulate a response. The mentor, however, should be sensitive to the feelings of the pupil at this point as equally, the pupil may interpret the silence as lack of interest or disapproval on the part of the mentor. If the pupil is uncomfortable with the silence, a series of prompts could be used to encourage the pupil to re-engage in the conversation.

Reflecting back – To show understanding – through paraphrasing and picking out the most important detail of what has been said – the mentor can reassure the pupil that what they have said has been heard and understood. By summarising what has been said the mentor clarifies what has been said and puts it into a more organised format that gives the pupil a clearer picture of the situation.

Discussions at times can seem difficult to handle. The mentor may become embarrassed by the way a conversation is developing, especially as some youngsters deliberately set out to shock with their revelations. Equally, the pupils may find some topics painful or difficult to discuss and so the mentors need to be ready to change the topic of discussion and plan to revisit it at a future meeting if they feel the necessity. Where the mentor is not wholly up-to-date with current jargon of youth culture they must explain this to the pupil rather than allowing a misunderstanding to happen. In turn, mentors need to ensure that they do not use jargon or language that is not understood by the pupil. If technical words are used, then they need to be explained (particularly when talking to parents) as it is important that the language used does not make them feel inferior or inadequate. All of these are considerations that need to be taken into account.

When working with a child it is important for the Learning Mentor to assess the ability of the child to listen. If they are tired or unwell their ability to listen will be impaired. If this is the case it may be wise to postpone the interview rather than risk the pupil–mentor relationship. Where the pupil may have frequently experienced failure in lessons, they will need a lot of patient coaxing until they have an open mind about options in any given situation. They are also likely to pre-judge situations and hear only what they wish to hear in any conversation. It is here where skilled questioning should be used to ascertain the feelings of the child in respect to their learning and perception of life in school as a whole.

Types of conversations

In casual conversation, people rarely analyse what they are saying, they merely indulge in what is usually an enjoyable type of social interaction. Conversations between Learning Mentors and pupils are about getting pupils to open up and talk about their concerns, to have better insight into their barriers to learning and to look at how they may solve them. Learning Mentors need to develop a range of communication skills in order to effectively communicate with and support the pupils.

Closed questions should be used when an answer to a specific question is required, as only a 'yes' or 'no' is required in response and this can be useful to establish facts. Open questions, on the other hand, encourage exploration or discussion of an issue and they will help the mentor to get a feel about the pupil's interpretation of a problem. These could be followed for example by more probing questions to get the pupil to focus more carefully on particular issues.

One of the greatest difficulties encountered by a Learning Mentor is the non-responsive, silent pupil. The pupil may be being defensive, or may merely find talking difficult. It is here where the mentor needs to have a range of strategies at hand, otherwise there is a chance that the mentoring relationship could well break down. Some pupils find it easier to explain ideas in writing or through diagrams, and this should be explored as a possibility.

Responding to conversation is crucial to the way in which the mentor is perceived and trusted by a pupil. It is therefore important that the true nature of a conversation is understood. It is said by doctors that patients often only reveal what is troubling them in a 'throwaway'comment as they are leaving the surgery. This is an important factor. It is vital to pick up on information offered whether it be overt or covert. Even more important is the response from the Learning Mentor. The following examples demonstrate such responses:

Sharing information/experiences	Emily comes to find her Learning Mentor and wants to discuss a technology lesson. She is pleased with her project work and wants to share her feeling of achievement.
	All she requires of the mentor is that she gets the mentor's full attention, approval and praise. The mentor should try to find time to respond as soon as possible so that the mentee does not feel rejected.

Understanding and empathy	Sabina is clearly upset. She has been crying in her lesson and wants to go home. Her pet dog died at the weekend. She needs the mentor to listen sensitively and show that she understands the way that Sabina is feeling at the moment. Through such understanding, the mentor will probably be able to keep Sabina in school.
Enabling	Daniel wants you to help him decide about his future. He wants to be a sports instructor. He's good at PE, and goes training in the gym every evening, so claims that he hasn't got time to do homework. Daniel needs the mentor to help him access careers information and specialist help. He also needs help with time management. He must then come to a decision himself about his priorities.
Supporting and encouraging	Neil is upset. His examinations are imminent but he cannot concentrate because he is either with his girlfriend or thinking about her. He needs six good exam passes to get into college. He is getting into a mess. The mentor must show that s/he understands and is non-judgemental about the relationship. S/he needs to help Neil understand what his options are and support him as he comes to a decision.

The referral process

Referral processes tend to be unique to each school and reflect the organisation's preferred way of working. Some Learning Mentors have complained about being stopped in the corridor and asked to 'sort out John' who is clearly driving a teacher to distraction. Such incidents are fortunately becoming rarer as a result of each school's staff being made more aware of the true role of the Learning Mentor. The referral process enables the Learning Mentor to prioritise their work and plan ahead. This is particularly important when issue-based group work is going to be undertaken.

Figure 4.3 is shown to demonstrate the process devised by the Learning Mentor at Perry Beeches Secondary school in Birmingham from the pupil's referral to exit.

Action

One-to-one

The Learning Mentor has to make decisions about the nature of discussions that they wish to hold with their pupils. There are times when one-to-one meetings will be the most suitable as intensive work may need to be undertaken on an issue such as anger management or developing organizational skills, or when supporting a pupil with some personal problem that is preventing them from learning.

During the first session the Learning Mentor explains the mentoring process and discusses the potential benefits of the partnership. A timescale is established from

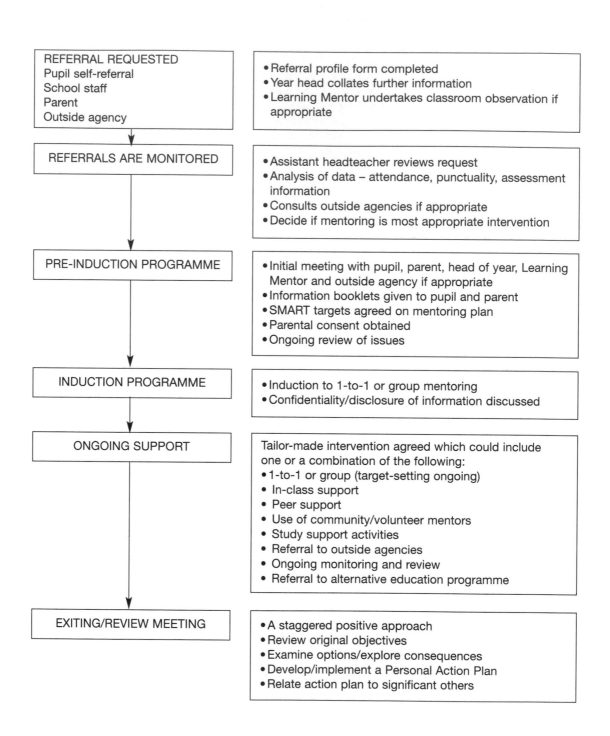

Figure 4.3 Referral and mentoring strategy at Perry Beeches School

**Shireland Language College
Learning Mentor Team**

Mentoring Agreement

The aim of this Mentoring Partnership is to provide support, guidance and encouragement to students in order to help them overcome barriers that may be affecting their progress in college.

On this basis, we (the student and the mentor) agree to the following:

- **To meet when agreed**
- **To be respectful of each other**
- **To listen to each other**
- **To be open and honest**
- **To respect appropriate confidentiality**
- **To be willing to learn from each other**
- **To share knowledge and ideas**
- **To review our progress regularly**

Mentor:.........................(Name) ....(Signed)

Student:.........................(Name) ....(Signed)

Date:...........

Figure 4.4 Mentoring agreement
Source: Adapted from *The Good Practice Guidelines for Learning Mentors* (DfES 2001)

the outset – this does not have to be written in 'tablets of stone' and can of course be adjusted if necessary. A mentor agreement may be signed which highlights the need for mutual respect and honesty (see Figure 4.4). It is also possible that a self-assessment form (such as those produced by NFER) may be completed by the pupil and discussions can then be centred around strengths and weaknesses, out of school interests and activities and achievements. Engaging in some practical activities might also be used to give the pupil time to settle into the situation.

Many mentors work with the pupils in 6 to 7 weekly sessions with half-termly targets being set at the start of the mentoring programme, and weekly more specific targets set to help them work towards their longer term goals. Figure 4.5 gives an example of a fivefold process that may typically ensue:

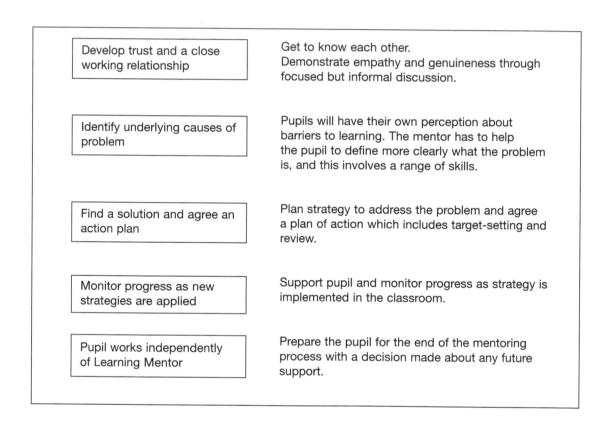

Figure 4.5 A five-stage model of the mentoring process

As part of this process, mentoring record sheets should be completed. An example of such a sheet is given in Figure 4.6.

PERRY BEECHES SCHOOL STUDENT SUPPORT DEPARTMENT

Excellence in Cities Aiming to Achieve Mentoring Programme

MENTORING RECORD SHEET

Student's name _____ Form _____

Mentor/Organization _____ Date _____

Lesson   1   2   3   4   5   6   Subject Missed _____

Targets _____

_____

_____

Progress made towards targets:-
New/modified targets/comments:-
Student's comments (Did you benefit from this session? How?):-

FT	YT	????	?????	Student support CO	SENCO	ESW	School nurse	OTHER

Figure 4.6 An individual mentoring record sheet

Small group meetings

Pupils allocated to small groups are normally characterised by a commonality of experience such as victims of bullying/poor attenders/young carers/pupils at risk. These pupils may need to share information, for example smoking/alcohol awareness. They may also be involved in group sessions that focus on specific issues such as study/key skills, revision skills or social interaction. Once again, time limits have to be set.

As a variation of this work, in primary schools Learning Mentors often run lunchtime activities to help pupils who find it difficult to cope with the unstructured nature of the lunch break.

> One primary Learning Mentor, having noted that some children were having problems controlling themselves at lunchtime and were in danger of becoming excluded from school at lunchtime, established a lunchtime Friendship Club. Pupils were invited to join the club, and through a series of social activities learnt skills of participation, how to interact positively with others and make new friends. The group also had access to computers and were able to learn ICT skills. As a consequence of this intervention, only one child in the year group had to be excluded from school at lunchtime.

Although pupils who are working together in a small group are likely to have a commonality of experience they may not have met prior to becoming part of the group. In order that open discussion can take place, it is important that the group sets and agrees ground rules for itself, and the Learning Mentor has to facilitate this. The most important of these rules is confidentiality, and an understanding that they can speak freely without the fear that anything they say will be common knowledge in the playground before the end of the day. Without this guarantee the children may not engage fully in the session. Other possible rules suggested by primary school children included:

We must listen to each other.
Only one person talks at a time.
Don't make fun of what anyone says.
No put-downs are allowed.
You don't have to speak if you don't want to.
Help one another.
Show respect to everyone.

Some group work will tend to be more active than others and the development of the skills of working in pairs and threes will have to be fostered. The Learning Mentor may need to enable the pupils to develop such skills in order for them to work effectively together. A good example of this is assertiveness training groups, where a high degree of interaction is required.

Records should be kept of all such group sessions, and the participants given an opportunity to reflect on their contribution (Figure 4.7).

PERRY BEECHES SCHOOL STUDENT SUPPORT DEPARTMENT

Excellence in Cities Aiming to Achieve Mentoring Programme

GROUP MENTORING RECORD SHEET

Student's name and form _____

Mentor/Organization _____ Date _____

Lesson   1   2   3   4   5   6 Subject Missed _____

Session Objective _____

_____

Observations/Comments/Assessment of group (based on objective): -

Student's comments (Did you benefit from this session? How?): -

FT	YT	????	?????	Student support CO	SENCO	ESW	School nurse	OTHER

Figure 4.7 A group mentoring record sheet

Using circle time, where the pupils sit in a circle to show that they are all equal and everyone has an equal chance to take part, has proved to be very effective for dealing with a wide range of situations – some of which could be quite contentious. Once again, for control, and to ensure whole group participation, ground rules must be agreed. As the pupils take it in turn to speak in response to prompts or a previously agreed agenda it is important that everyone listens without comment. Circle time provides the pupils with a chance to explore issues of shared concern and most certainly helps to develop relationships.

Self-referral/drop-in provision

Learning Mentors are often instrumental in organising social learning occasions where they are available for 'casual conversation'. Lunchtime clubs, breakfast clubs or homework clubs can prove to be very well supported; in fact, many Learning Mentors face the difficulty of having to limit numbers due to popularity. These sessions give youngsters the possibility to self-refer, or give the mentor a chance to alert staff to a need. It further gives an opportunity for pupils who have been through the exit process from a formal programme to maintain an informal link with their mentor.

Some mentors make a point of having lunch in the canteen, where the children have easy opportunity for informal contact. Many Learning Mentors organise extra-curricular activities for pupils, sometimes across the school; for example, year 7 football or a Scrabble club. These may sometimes be specifically for the pupils being mentored. In addition to this, being at the school gates at the start and end of the day gives an opportunity for further conversations, and this may be with the pupils and/or their parents. Outside of school, residential visits are especially popular and give the pupils a chance to experience success and develop personal and social skills in a whole new environment.

In primary schools it is particularly important that the Learning Mentor is visible in the playground. It provides a great opportunity for informal contact and chat and also allows discreet observation of playground behaviour. Some children find playtime an extremely stressful time and they will need help and support in overcoming their difficulties. In some cases this may require directed training in social skills. Teaching children new games to play for example can reduce boredom while at the same time developing their social interaction. Conflicts often occur in the playground and bullies come into their own, so observation helps in identifying those children who are causing the problems and those who are the victims. When taking up issues that have arisen from playground observation, the Learning Mentor needs to formalise strategies with respect to taking action, and processes used for recording discussions need to be adhered to.

Working with parents/carers

Parents/carers are key partners in the learning process and it is important that

Learning Mentors get to know them; however, they need to be aware of the specific context of the family and any legal orders that may be in place:

The Children Act 1989

It is essential that schools are aware of the family circumstances of their pupils, especially where pupils do not live with both their natural parents. The Children Act defines who has *parental responsibility* for the child, and that person then assumes all the rights, duties, powers, responsibilities and authority that a parent of a child has by law. Both married parents or an unmarried mother automatically have parental responsibility and continue to have it even if they separate or divorce. They can only lose this as the result of an adoption order.

Further guidance is provided about

- **Specific issue order** – which gives directions on how a specific issue in relation to the exercise of parental responsibility is to be decided. This would, for example, allow a parent to agree to a pupil changing school against the wishes of the other parent.
- **Prohibited steps order** – which forbids the exercise of parental responsibility in a particular way. This would allow one parent to prevent a child from attending a form of religious worship against the wishes of the other parent.
- **Residence order** – which says where and with whom a child should live.
- **Contact order** – instructs the person with whom the child is living to allow the child to visit or stay with the person named in the order, or have contact by letter or telephone.

The mentor must remain non-judgemental when considering the family circumstances, and be wary at the same time of being drawn into any debate about the parenting skills of either party. The school must treat all those with parental responsibility equally. This means that care must be taken to ensure that parents living separately receive the same information and opportunities to be involved in their child's education.

In cases where a child is being looked after by a foster carer or is living in a children's home, although the birth parents continue to have parental responsibility, this may be restricted in terms of actual contact with their child. Whatever the situation, it is the day-to-day carers, and the child's caseworker, that need to be kept informed about the child's progress, and they will usually notify all other interested parties.

It is important to gain parental permission prior to embarking on the mentoring process. Most schools have a standard letter to send. The letter should clearly state the role of the mentor and the nature and purpose of the mentoring sessions. Parents should be invited to meet with the mentor at school if they have any concerns that they wish to discuss. It is usual for the pupil to be present at any meeting with the parent or carer, and if this is not the case the child must be told why they are not being invited.

Kings Norton High School
Learning Mentor Support Service

PARENTAL CONSULTATION

Date: .... Venue: ....

Name of Parent/Carer: ....

Purpose of Consultation: ....

Consultation Overview:

Summary/Action

Figure 4.8 A parental consultation record sheet

**Kings Norton High School
Learning Mentor Support Service**

TELEPHONE CONTACT SHEET

Date: .... Time: ....

Making call to/returning call of/receiving call from: ....

Call made by: ....

Regarding:

Summary/Action

Figure 4.9 Telephone contact record sheet

Notes should be kept of any meeting with parents whether it be at a Parents' Evening, individual interview or home visit (Figure 4.8). Much day-to-day information exchange and discussion of progress is often done by telephone, but it is equally important that a written summary is kept of these discussions (Figure 4.9). Parents' groups have proved to be popular, whereby a group of parents with similar concerns meet together with the Learning Mentor to discuss their concerns in a semi-formal meeting.

Home visits

Learning Mentors should be available to meet with parents at school events such as parents' evenings or social gatherings. Occasionally the Learning Mentor may feel that a home visit would be helpful, in which case school guidance must be followed. Many schools have Home–School Liaison Workers and it may be more appropriate for them to make the visit on behalf of the Learning Mentor, or for a joint visit to be undertaken.

The school will be able to offer advice about any issues relating to the family that may be pertinent to the visit being made. The Education Welfare Officer or Home–School Liaison Worker may also have relevant information to offer. In particular the Learning Mentor needs to know whether there has been any history of violence or aggression in relationships between the school and the family from the viewpoint of their own safety.

Protocol for home visits

- Do a risk assessment in relation to the visit.
- Make sure that the line manager or school knows that the visit is taking place.
- Carry a mobile phone.
- Ensure that parents'/carers' correct names are known.
- Agree a mutually convenient time for the meeting.
- Be sensitive to any cultural traditions within the home.
- Accept whatever situation you find yourself in – conversations may be undertaken with the television full on and the baby crawling at your feet!
- Inform the line manager when the visit has been completed.
- Fill in a parental interview sheet.

If the visit has been successful, every effort should be made to ensure that the positive link is maintained. Parents' understanding of their children's progress is crucial to a successful partnership between the school and home. Once the initial contact has been made with the family in their home, those who were previously reluctant to visit the school may now have the confidence to do so.

When visits are made to the homes of ethnic minority parents, it is essential that communication is made possible in the home language of the family, and if necessary, an interpreter should accompany the mentor on the visit. There is also a need to be aware of any cultural norms that may apply.

Child protection

> The welfare of the child shall be the paramount consideration.
>
> Children Act

The Children Act 1989 places duties on various agencies, including school, to assist local authority social services acting on behalf of children in need or enquiring into allegations of abuse. Adults working with children must be able to recognise suspected child abuse and know what action to take. The teacher/mentor role is to 'act on suspicion' – the investigative role is undertaken by the police or social services. Great care must therefore be taken when talking to children who are disclosing possible abuse. Leading questions should not be asked as they may invalidate testimony in court. Prompting children could be interpreted as putting words into the child's mouth. A trusted Learning Mentor, especially in informal settings, might be the first person to whom the child talks about their private life. A promise of confidentiality must never be given and this needs to be made clear to the child from the outset.

The Children Act exists to protect young people and a child's word will always be taken seriously. This will identify malicious allegations as well as genuine ones. Any adult working with young people needs to be aware that well meant actions may be misinterpreted or misunderstood and so it is in their interest not to put themselves at risk of allegations of abuse.

All Learning Mentors will have received training on Child Protection issues. Figures 4.10, 4.11, and 4.12 outline some of the practical considerations that will have been raised in training and may act as an aide memoire.

Having considered working with both pupils and their families, and taking account of the needs of the child, it is clear that in this working relationship, the Learning Mentor may well, at times, need to access additional support. It is here we look towards working with outside agencies.

Emotional abuse: this occurs where a child consistently faces a lack of love and affection or is constantly threatened by verbal attacks, taunting and shouting.

Young people who have been emotionally abused may seem sad, cry a lot and display apathetic or aggressive behaviour. They may have a lack of confidence and low self-esteem.

Physical Abuse: where a child is physically hurt. It can involve hitting, shaking, squeezing, burning and biting. It also involves giving a child poisonous substances, inappropriate drugs and alcohol.

Physical abuse can leave obvious signs e.g. bruising, burns, fractures and cuts, all without reasonable explanation or cause.

DEFINITIONS

Neglect: where parents/carers fail to meet the basic and essential needs of their young people like food, appropriate clothes, warmth and medical care. Leaving children alone is another form of abuse.

Children who have been neglected suffer a number of difficulties. They seem unusually withdrawn and miserable, they may be over-aggressive, have eating disorders, be dirty and/or smelly.

Sexual abuse: when young people are exploited sexually by adults who use them to meet their own needs. It includes intercourse, fondling, masturbation, oral sex and exposing young people to pornographic material, including videos.

Youngsters who have been sexually abused often become depressed or withdrawn, may display unusually aggressive behaviour, may have eating disorders or have relationships with adults which exclude others. They may display or talk about sexual behaviour which is inappropriate for their age.

CHILD PROTECTION

CONFIDENTIALITY

Learning Mentors cannot promise confidentiality to pupils who make allegations of abuse. They have a professional responsibility to share relevant information with the designated teacher in school. It is essential that Learning Mentors do not make promises that they cannot keep, especially before they know what is to be confided. The child must not feel that their trust has been breached and must be assured that the matter will only be discussed on a need-to-know basis.

CHILD PROTECTION OFFICER

Each school should have a member of staff who is the designated teacher for matters relating to Child Protection. The role of the teacher includes:

- Ensuring all staff (teaching and non-teaching) are familiar with child protection issues
- Ensuring all staff are aware of who is the designated member of staff
- Monitoring child protection procedures in school
- Maintaining a record of children in the school who are on the Child Protection Register and monitoring their progress
- Ensuring that all cases of suspected abuse are reported to the appropriate agency
- Taking part in case conferences and reviews where appropriate
- Offering support to staff who are involved in a child protection case

Figure 4.10 Child Protection: key concepts

Learning mentors may become involved by
• Being told something by a pupil • Overhearing a conversation, or someone else reporting a concern • Seeing an injury which causes concern, or an inconsistent reason given for its origin • Having concern about a child over a period of time • Noticing a deterioration in behaviour, a change in personality or a change in appearance

If a child makes a disclosure
• Listen to the child and respond with sensitivity • Do not make judgements or take sides • Do not interrogate – merely ask sufficient questions to establish whether there is a cause for concern • Do not promise confidentiality As soon as possible, make notes about the disclosure – use the child's words – do not interpret or paraphrase. Date your statement – it may be used in court as evidence.

Action
Refer concerns to the designated teacher for child protection. The case will then be passed on to the experts and they will decide what action to take.

Figure 4.11 Becoming involved in child protection concerns

Physical Contact	Relationships outside school
• As a general principle mentors should not make unnecessary physical contact. • There may be times when a distressed child may need comfort and reassurance and a mentor may offer physical comfort as a caring parent would. • Children may find being touched uncomfortable for a variety of reasons. It is important that a mentor is sensitive to a child's reaction to physical contact and acts appropriately. It is also important not to touch pupils, however casually, in ways or at parts of the body that may be considered indecent.	• Extra-curricular activities – parents should be aware of these; there should be another adult present • Home visits – follow school guidance • If you regularly receive cards, gifts, etc. from pupils, report this to a line manager

AVOIDING ALLEGATIONS OF ABUSE

Transporting pupils	Meetings/interviews with children
• Car drivers should ensure that they have another adult in the car where possible if transporting young people. The youngster should sit in the back. • A minibus driver should have another adult in the minibus.	• Learning mentors should ensure that their manner and language is always appropriate in front of children. • Use a room which is open to view from the outside and is in a commonly used part of the school. • Inform colleagues that a meeting is taking place. • Do not sit in a position which makes a child feel that the exit to the room is blocked.

Figure 4.12 Avoiding allegations of abuse

5 Working with outside agencies

The work of the Learning Mentor involves dealing with pupils who have a wide range of needs. There will be those children whose needs are met by the facilities and staff within the school. Conversely, there will be those who require additional support that is beyond the scope of the school. In light of this, an awareness of the work of outside agencies or services is required in order to access appropriate specialist help.

Schools will have their own referral mechanisms and are likely to have named members of staff who act as a contact point for specific referrals. For example, where attendance is an issue it may be a designated Head of Year, where learning difficulties are an issue it will be the SENCO (Special Educational Needs Co-ordinator). In order to achieve a harmonious working relationship, the Learning Mentor should find out the school contact(s) and familiarise themselves with procedures for referral ensuring that they work within the guidelines and boundaries laid down.

Accessing additional support is all well and good if there is a sound understanding of the range available outside of the school. It is with this in mind that the information in this chapter aims to provide a brief synopsis of some of the people or agencies that schools may have to access if faced with particular issues and problems.

What happens if I suspect a child has a specific difficulty that requires some form of assessment?

The first port of call here must be the SENCO, for it is s/he who will have access to the expertise within school to make an initial assessment. This is often done by themselves or within the Special Educational Needs Department.

Upon completion of the assessment, the SENCO will provide information on the child and, if there is a need, provide an individual education plan for that child. It is here that a whole process begins, which involves target-setting, evaluation and review. Where the school is unable to discover from assessment the needs of the child, then a range of outside agencies may be called upon.

LEAs may have both Learning and Behaviour Support teams who are available to their schools for advice, assessment and teaching. Where these are not available, the LEA may be able to provide names and contact numbers or addresses of similar organisations. Funding for external input comes from within the school's delegated budget. It is the school's responsibility to 'buy in' when the need arises. Where such teams recommend identified support, the SENCO may call upon a range of specialists to advise or teach and these may include, for example, personnel with expertise in

- Speech and Language Therapy
- Hearing Impairment
- Visual Impairment
- Emotional and Behavioural Difficulties
- Cognitive Difficulties, e.g. dyslexia, dyscalculia, dyspraxia
- Occupational Therapy

Further to such professionals, there may be the need to ascertain whether the child is in need of additional support that may require a more formal assessment to identify if the child requires the protection of a 'statement of special educational need'. Where this decision is taken, the SENCO will request further assessments from the following, who must provide information on the child's abilities and a written report including recommendations:

- *Educational Psychologist* – performs specialised assessments that can only be administered by a qualified EP.
- *Health Service* – provides an assessment of the well-being of the child and provides appropriate, related advice. This may include, for example, the child's General Practitioner, a Community Paediatrician, the Child and Adolescent Mental Health Service (CAMHS).
- *Social Services* – provide a report on the child's 'situation' and make appropriate recommendations (where the child is known to them).
- *Educational Welfare Officer* – where attendance may be an issue a report may identify reasons, action previously taken and recommendations.

In addition to these external agencies/services, advice will be asked of the school, parents and any other personnel who have been involved with the child.

This is a very brief 'whistle stop tour' of those professionals involved with special educational needs issues and provision. It is by no means exhaustive, as within each area there is a range of personnel who may become involved. There is a need for the mentor to understand from the outset that, where identifiable learning difficulties that may be related to a special educational need are a cause for concern, the SENCO should be informed immediately.

What happens when I need information or support with regard to a child whose poor attendance is affecting their achievement?

The Learning Mentor in a secondary school would most likely approach the designated Head of Year/Head of Key Stage for the identified pupil. In a primary school it is more likely to be a Deputy Headteacher or the Headteacher.

The school will have mechanisms for dealing with attendance issues and the designated person will be able to offer support and guidance on related issues. There may, however, be times when the mentor requires additional support with specific issues that relate to the role of the Attendance Officer or Education Welfare Officer. The question is, what is their role and when do they become involved?

Each school should have an attached Education Welfare Officer or Attendance Officer, who is part of the wider Education Welfare Service. The role of the EWO, as described by one LEA, is summed up by the Service's mission statement.

The Education Welfare Service will endeavour to ensure that all children are given the opportunity to benefit from efficient full time education suitable to their age, ability and aptitude and any special education needs they may have, through attendance at school or otherwise. To achieve this the Education Welfare Service will strive for excellence through training and development and by working in partnership with schools, governors, families and other agencies.

The Education Welfare Officer will, on behalf of the EWS:

- fulfil the duty of the LEA to enforce school attendance and where necessary institute legal proceedings;
- endeavour to ensure that all children are able to benefit fully from the educational opportunities that are open to them;
- seek to prevent the exploitation of children in employment and entertainment;
- work together with schools and other agencies to protect children from abuse;
- co-operate with schools and agencies in addressing problems which affect children within society, e.g. crime, drugs, alcohol, gambling;
- endeavour to ensure equality of access to services and assist in addressing the many disadvantages which may limit the pupils' ability to develop their full potential;
- help to enable the families of children at school to receive the material benefits to which they are entitled.

So, why would the Learning Mentor need access to the EWO? Research has indicated that absence has more effect on pupil progress than any other single factor. In light of this, it is important for the Learning Mentor to establish a positive working relationship with the school's EWO. This will allow for a greater impact upon those pupils who, for one reason or another, are not attending school. It should be remembered, however, that the designated person in charge of the pupil's attendance should be kept fully informed of any action taken by either the mentor or the EWO to ensure a whole school approach. The child and their parents/carers would not welcome 'overkill' and this may in fact only serve to alienate them further from the school.

What happens when the Connexions service becomes involved with a pupil?

The first point is that this should not come as a surprise to you! The Connexions service Personal Advisers work within schools and engage with young people in a variety of ways, but their work should further complement all the other work being undertaken with young people in schools. The Personal Adviser works with students from 13 to 19 and thus should be known to all youngsters from year 8 onwards. The Personal Adviser, like the Learning Mentor, may work with youngsters in small groups or on a one-to-one basis but their focus is on working with young people to help them make decisions about their future and offer advice on routes into employment, training or further education. If during discussion they come across obstacles that are reducing the chances of the young person engaging successfully in education or training post-16 they will draw on expertise and help young people access appropriate help. Some Personal Advisers have specialist knowledge of the needs of young people with learning difficulties and disabilities.

Personal Advisers thus are another valuable resource for Learning Mentors, and many already work closely together. At its simplest, having a longer-term view of what skills and qualifications they need in order to follow a particular career helps motivate some youngsters, and the link between the personal adviser and a pupil is likely to be longer-term than that between the mentor and the pupil. The personal adviser has specialist knowledge of training and employment within a particular region and has time to liaise with external agencies such as colleges and training providers, and it is essential that Key Stage 4 students are able to access such information. They also have access to a range of alternative curriculum providers and can support the work of Learning Mentors in finding placements for students who would benefit from such alternative provision.

What do I need to know about Looked After Children (LAC)/Children in Public Care?

The term 'Looked After Children' applies to the large group of children who are cared for by the local authority. It was introduced by the Children Act 1989 and refers to children who are subject to care orders and those who are 'accommodated' by the local authority. Those with care orders have parental responsibility shared between their parents and the local authority.

Each school should have a member of staff who is the designated teacher for 'Looked After Children'. The role of this teacher will include:

- being an advocate for LAC
- accessing services and support
- ensuring that the school has high expectations for the LAC

- liaising with Social Services
- ensuring that a Personal Education Plan exists
- enabling transfer of information between agencies.

The last statistical analysis (quoted in DfEE *Guidance* 2000) showed 55,300 children and young people being looked after by local authorities in England: 65 per cent live in foster placements, 12 per cent in children's homes and the rest live in other residential provision or with their families with social worker support. The *Guidance* further explains:

> Children will enter public care for a variety of reasons. Many will have been affected by distressing and damaging experiences, including physical and sexual abuse and neglect. Some will be in public care because of the illness or death of a parent, or because their families are in some way unable to provide adequate care for them. The majority of young people in public care come from families who experience hardship and are separated from them because of some form of family upheaval or breakdown. Less that 2 per cent of young people are in public care because of offences they have committed.

Two distinct groups of young people are looked after. The larger group are in stable placements with foster carers or in small children's homes that provide high quality care, and, although a substantial number are not achieving at the expected level for their age, they are assessed within the schools as functioning at a level which is reasonable given their abilities. The second group includes children who are frequently moved from one placement to another, who react badly to change, or who are in children's homes where high standards are difficult to achieve. These children underachieve, truant and are at risk of exclusion.

While each young person's experience is unique, various barriers to educational success have been identified with respect to Looked After Children who may:

- experience numerous, unplanned moves of home and as a result have to move to a new school: difficulties often encountered when a new school place is sought for them;
- have difficulty making and sustaining relationships with peers. This can pose particular problems because they have to keep making new friends as they change schools;
- experience low self-esteem and have a mistrust of adults;
- have had a lack of continuity in care providers and teachers, meaning that they cannot rely upon familiar adults who they feel able to trust and who will help them;
- have not had a good multi-agency approach to them, and so important information has not been shared;
- be proportionally over-represented among pupils who are excluded from school.

To try and alleviate some of these difficulties, all looked after children are required to have a Personal Education Plan (PEP) which will help track their educational progress and ensure effective transfer of information between schools. PEPs are drawn up by the social worker and the designated teacher at the school and are reviewed every six months.

Many examples of good practice have been identified in *Raising Achievement of Children in Public Care* (Ofsted 2001).

What happens if a girl tells me she is pregnant?

There are a number of issues here that need to be taken into account:

- Does the girl's parent/carer know?
- Does anyone else in the school know?
- Have they spoken to any professionals seeking advice?
- Have they had medical attention?
- Are there any child protection implications?

Learning Mentors in secondary schools may well, at one time or another, find that they are faced with dealing with this situation. It is most definitely a major issue with respect to pupil achievement as stated in the *Report on Teenage Pregnancy* (Social Exclusion Unit, 1999) which stated:

Teenage mothers are less likely to finish their education, less likely to find a good job, and more likely to end up both as single parents and bringing up their children in poverty.

Britain has the highest rate of teenage pregnancy in Western Europe. DfES Circular 11/99 advises LEAs to work with schools and social services departments to support pupils at school during pregnancy. Their aim is to keep the pupils involved in education and to remain on the school roll during this period, to enable them to return to school after the birth should they choose to do so. The nature of educational provision will vary between LEAs but may include initiatives such as providing home tuition and specialist units, prior to a return to school or college.

Specialist units provide a combination of education, childcare and support in the development of parenting skills. Best practice responds to individual need and allows the girls to continue with their school courses, including GCSEs, if appropriate. Additionally, the girls receive guidance on parenting skills, careers, preparation for continuing education, the world of work and independent living.

Learning Mentors should familiarise themselves with provision in their own areas so that they are able to talk in confidence to their mentee about what is available to them.

They should also be aware that teenage fathers are sometimes overlooked, and yet they may need considerable emotional support, as well as information about some of the practicalities of pregnancy.

Whatever the response to the above, where the girl has decided to have the baby she will need to have information on her rights to future education and it is here where the Learning Mentor can provide information on what options are available to the girl both during the pregnancy and after the birth of the child.

What happens when asylum seekers/refugees join the school?

Asylum seekers are people who flee their home country and seek refugee status in another country. A person is recognised as a refugee when the government decides they meet the UN definition of a refugee and accepts that the person has a well-founded fear of being persecuted. A person with refugee status is granted indefinite leave to remain in the UK.

Asylum-seeking pupils come from many countries, and while most come to the UK with one or both parents, some do not. They may arrive with friends or relatives who are not their normal carers, or they may arrive as unaccompanied asylum-seeking children. Asylum-seeking and refugee children have a wide range of education and social needs that may relate to

- an interrupted education in their country of origin
- horrific experiences in their home country and flight to the UK, and for a small number this may affect their ability to learn and to rebuild their lives
- suffering a drop in their standard of living and other major changes in their lives
- not being cared for by their parents or usual carers
- having parents who are emotionally absent
- living with families who do not know their educational or social rights
- speaking little or no English on arrival in the UK
- suffering racist bullying or isolation in school

Learning Mentors working in schools where asylum seekers/refugees are attending need to be aware that these issues will most definitely impact upon their ability to learn. Extra funding has been allocated to such schools and, in addition to available in-school resources, help might also be accessed through the LEA's Ethnic Minority Support Service.

What happens if I or the school do not have appropriate expertise to offer appropriate advice or support?

It is here where voluntary agencies and charitable organisations should be investigated. There is a vast range of services available 'out there' providing support and guidance on a whole range of issues. Figure 5.1 demonstrates, for example, some of those that can be accessed in Birmingham. Other cities will equally have information available on accessing additional support including the type, range and contact information.

Where volunteer mentors are concerned, co-ordination of their work is generally accepted as one of the roles of the Learning Mentor. Many volunteer mentors work with pupils in the schools at the request of the Learning Mentor and many have specialist skills to offer. Volunteer mentors for example can be accessed in Birmingham through organisations such as Mentor Access Point and Second City; Second Chance with the security of knowing that the mentors will have undergone the necessary police checks and initial training. Mentors range from university

Cruse – support for the bereaved

Kwesi – African-Caribbean support

Second City Second Chance – mentoring and training

Refugee Council

University of the First Age – Training/"Gifted and Talented" activities

Big Brothers and Sisters – single parent families

Barnardo's – child abuse/prostitution

Care Included – Children In Public Care

Parents for Prevention – drug/solvent misuse

Mentor Access Point – volunteer mentors

100 Black Men – mentors/role models

West Midlands Traveller Education Consortium

Young Carers – children caring for family members

Valued Youth Programme – cross age tutoring

Ambassadors – role models

St Basil's – work with the homeless

Kidscape – support for bullies/victims and their families

NSPCC – guidance on child protection and peer support

Pioneers – Bangladeshi /Pakistani mentors

Alternative curriculum providers /trainers

Birmingham Women's Aid – domestic violence

Figure 5.1 Accessing specialist support

students who may support academic mentoring, mentors from particular ethnic groups who offer support to similar groups and mentors with specialist knowledge who can support pupils who have specific needs, e.g. mentors for children in care.

Serious consideration should also be given to local branches of charitable organisations such as NSPCC, Barnardos and Cruse, as they combine national expertise with the benefit of local knowledge and offer invaluable support to schools and parents. Local branches of the police, fire service and army contribute to support work with young people in schools in many spheres, including promotion of self-esteem, acting as role models and offering workshops on, for example, drug education. Learning Mentors tend to build up their own local directory of services and through networking quickly get to know those organisations which offer helpful advice.

What do I need to be aware of when working with Traveller children?

The phrase 'Travelling Communities' is used to cover those identifiable groups, some of which have minority ethnic status, who either are, or have been, traditionally associated with a nomadic lifestyle and include Gypsy Travellers, Fairground families (or Showpeople), Circus families, New Age Travellers, Bargees and other families living in boats. Of these, the Gypsy families are by far the largest group and constitute a recognised minority ethnic group for the purposes of the 1976 Race Relations Act.

Most of the groups have a positive attitude towards formal education and wish their children to have access to the acquisition of basic skills as a minimum. The children will lack continuity in their experience of schooling and so will need appropriate support with reintegration into the classroom. Learning Mentors will need to familiarise themselves with the cultural and social norms within the Traveller communities, especially those which could impinge on effective school performance. The children need to feel safe and welcomed within the school if they are to succeed.

An HMI report on the education of travelling children states:

> Travelling pupils appear to achieve higher standards in schools which place great emphasis on equality of opportunity and by encouraging the acceptance of cultural and ethnic diversity, establish an ethos which fosters self-esteem and pride in individual and group identity. Such a philosophy manifests itself through both the formal and informal curriculum.

Traveller Education Services provide support and advice for traveller children and may have their own peripatetic advisory and support teachers available, as well as resources which can be made available to the school.

What happens where a child is a young carer?

Young carers are children and young people who provide care for a sick or disabled relative at home. That person may have a physical disability or a mental health difficulty. The person they care for is often a parent, but it could be a grandparent or a brother or sister.

The young carer may be doing tasks like shopping, cooking or housework or they may be feeding, toileting and bathing their relative or providing emotional support. They may be getting help, or they may be doing all the caring alone if they have not spoken to anyone about their situation. The school may not realise that a child is a young carer as the child may be reluctant to talk about their situation. This is particularly true if their relative has an illness about which others may be prejudiced, such as schizophrenia, HIV/Aids or alcoholism.

Schools may be unaware that they have pupils who are young carers because they hide any problems that they face, fearing that if they admit to having problems, their parent may be seen as being unable to cope and they may be 'put into care'. In such circumstances they may work extra hard in order not to draw attention to themselves. Others may appear withdrawn, or have behaviour problems. The psychological effects on carers include problems relating to people and difficulty making friends. Many carers miss out on their childhood, which makes it difficult for them to adjust to situations when they are expected to behave like children, such as at school.

The national Young Carers organisation has local groups that can offer support to children. They are able, in a non-threatening way, to advise and help the youngster by, for example, offering practical help, respite care and giving them a chance to meet with other children in similar situations. They can talk to the school on the child's behalf.

Within the school it is important that there is a person to whom the child can speak openly about their difficulties at home. This may well be the Learning Mentor. The pupil's achievement may be adversely affected by their situation and so the school or Learning Mentor can offer some practical help. For example:

- It is clearly sometimes difficult for young carers to meet deadlines for schoolwork and allowances should be made for this. When respite care is made available, carers can meet socially with other young people who have similar responsibilities and so understandably school work may not always be a priority. Opportunities for study support should also be made available.
- Young carers may be late or absent from school because of their responsibilities. In a genuine crisis a school could approve absence until other arrangements can be made. A time limit should be set and the school should provide work.
- Many young carers would like to have access to a phone during the day to allay any fears they may have about the well-being of their relative. They may therefore need to have access to a private area where they could use the phone, or have permission to freely use their mobile phone in school.

Whatever support is offered, the child must feel at ease and able to cope with the situation otherwise additional stress may be placed upon them.

The range of support services covered in this chapter by no means gives the 'whole picture' as they are too numerous to mention. However, as mentioned earlier, the LEA should have a good database of such information. In addition to this, by 'surfing the Net', the Learning Mentor will have at their hand access to a wide range of contacts.

With this type of support mechanism in use, it should be possible for the mentor and indeed the school to ensure that all children are able to access learning and support. This is most important when we come to consider the equal opportunities and inclusion agenda.

6   Equal opportunities and inclusion

There has been extensive discussion about reasons why schools in similar areas have different degrees of success with the attainment of their pupils, and one outcome of this has been the Excellence in Cities initiative itself with its stress on achievement.

> Our aim is to drive up standards in our schools in the major cities higher and faster; to match the standards of excellence found in our best schools. The output must be that city parents and city children expect and gain as much from their schools as their counterparts anywhere else in the country. A vision of what city education can become is what Excellence in Cities is all about. Excellence must be the norm.

All schools have Equal Opportunities policies, guidance on dealing with incidents of racial and sexual harassment, etc. but unless these underpin the ethos of the school they will be perceived as worthless. Equality of opportunity should be integral to the whole school curriculum, and teaching should take account of the pupils' ethnicity and gender, as well as their preferred learning styles. Teaching should further promote a sense of worth by drawing on pupils' own experiences and encourage learning from different cultural experiences and traditions.

Learning Styles

Central to any child's achievement is the way in which they learn. Remember in Chapter 3 we looked at the Triune Brain and investigated the way in which the three distinct parts related to each other? We are now going to develop this understanding further and relate it to the impact upon learning – in relation to how we learn. Let us start by going back to the Thinking Cap, where all of the hard work takes place. What really does happen to enable us to take information on board, process it and use it in the future when needed? Figure 6.1 provides a mind map of the whole range of processing that may be involved, and although once again it is a brief synopsis it does provide some insight into the huge amount of work that goes on inside the brain. It most certainly highlights our need to consider the implications for the learner.

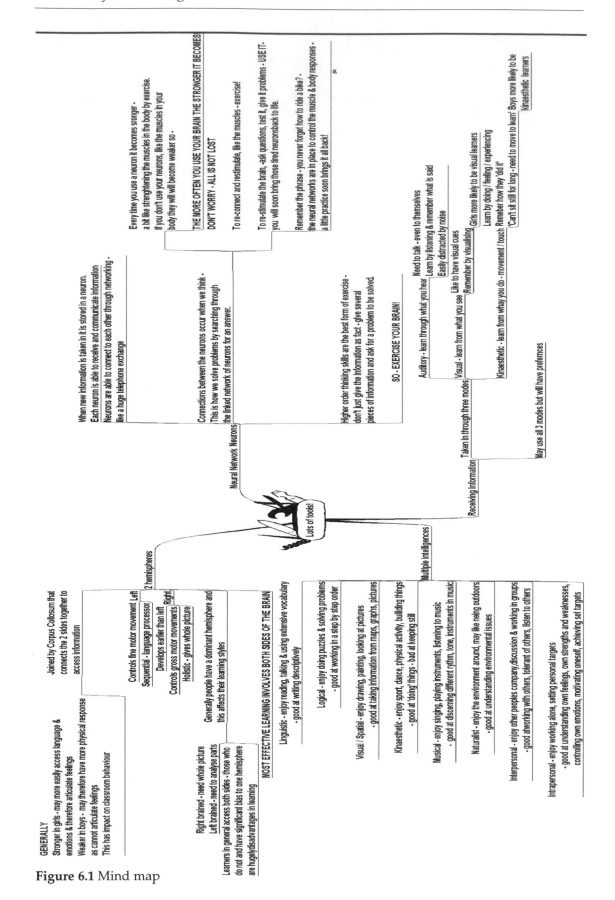

Figure 6.1 Mind map

You will have seen from certain parts of the mind map that there are implications for the way in which children learn. There are issues with left/right dominance, issues with differing intelligences, issues with the way in which learning is established through the transmission of messages, and issues with gender, and this is just a general overview! To put it into perspective, consider Figure 6.2 and ask the question set: Which of the pupils is likely to learn from the set work? If we analyse the information on the mind map it could well lead us towards a conclusion that the most likely pupil to learn would be Simon. However, we should still question the quality of his learning. Information taken in momentarily and not applied and reinforced will not be effectively retained.

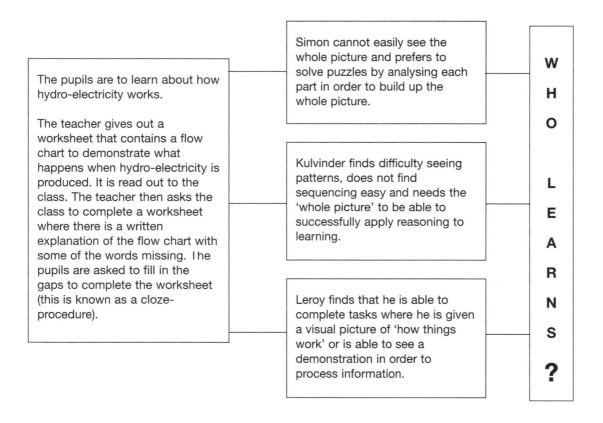

Figure 6.2 Who learns?

There are huge issues here when analysing what happens to children when learning. Perhaps the best way of gaining some understanding is to complete the following exercises for yourself:

EXERCISE 1
1. Remember an enjoyable lesson at school.
2. Think about the lesson content.
3. Write down the activities that you did.
4. What has helped your recall/memory.
5. Why did you enjoy the lesson?

EXERCISE 2
1. Remember a lesson you did not enjoy.
2. Can you remember the lesson content?
3. Can you remember the activities?
4. Why do you think you are having difficulty recalling?
5. Why do you think you didn't enjoy the lesson?

If you have taken time to do the above, you may well have discovered that you learned well when the teaching styles suited your own learning styles and learned far less when they did not. Take this one step further and ask yourself – did I have equality of opportunity?

Learning Mentors need to investigate the whole issue of teaching and learning styles in respect of accessing learning (see Additional reading). Those pupils who are not being offered a range of activities and tasks are most definitely not getting equality of opportunity. Interpreting from the mind map the information that is offered we can perhaps see that teaching styles in the classroom directed to the left brain, which do not take into account kinaesthetic learners and ignore the wider use of the intelligences, may well affect the behaviour of pupils. This could, in some instances, ultimately lead to exclusion. It is, however, a difficult situation for the Learning Mentor to deal with – teachers may be averse to changing their practice!

A further consideration for the Learning Mentor is the examination and testing system that puts pressure on many pupils. They most certainly do not take into account the range of learning styles, and those pupils struggling to cope with coursework and revision due to their particular learning styles may well need help in order to perform as effectively as possible. This is by no means an ideal solution but, at this moment in time, we cannot see the system changing, and therefore we have to work with the tools we have. It is here where study skills can be used to enable the pupils to analyse their learning preferences and help to apply them to the tasks in hand.

This brief simplistic look at the brain, its workings and the impact of learning and teaching styles has only gone a very short way to shedding some light on the difficulties children may face within school. Learning Mentors need to be aware that these difficulties could also bring with them the further burden of low self-esteem.

At this point, in relation to low self-esteem, it may well be appropriate to mention those pupils who have special educational needs. Many of these children may well perceive themselves as less able, stupid, useless, thick, hopeless (they will provide a multitude of descriptions), because of their difficulties with learning. Having looked at SEN earlier in the book there should be some awareness that schools do have systems in place, generally organised by the school's SENCO, to provide for equality of opportunity for such pupils, in line with the Code of Practice & Disability Act (DfES 2002). This may be in the form of resources, in-class support or specialist teaching. But, consider for one moment those pupils who do not respond to such input. Denial of a learning difficulty by a child could well result in:

- Reluctance or refusal to accept support
- Withdrawal or reticence in communicating
- Poor behaviour or exclusion
- Poor/non-attendance

If this is the case, input by a Learning Mentor could be crucial, particularly if the child sees the input as a friendly encounter in which they have equal status.

Other variables also impinge on a pupil's ability to achieve. DfEE guidance *Removing the Barriers* in its section on academic achievement states,

> Many schools found systematic and detailed ethnic monitoring an effective method for raising achievement levels. Ethnic monitoring was not viewed negatively as a way to stereotype children but as a way to identify learning problems and shortcomings in provision to make target setting more responsive'.

Monitoring by gender usually takes place alongside the ethnic monitoring, and the analysis of all such monitoring should inform policy and planning within school. Ideally, in addition to academic performance, the monitoring should cover aspects such as pupil behaviour, including bullying and harassment and exclusions; pupil attendance; allocations to subjects and ability groups; and parental and community involvement in the school; all of which are directly related to the work of the Learning Mentor.

The Gender Issue

The failure of boys to match the academic achievements of their female counterparts has long been a cause for concern and, as a consequence, much research has been undertaken to identify possible causes for this. Performance in English SATs tests show the girls outperforming the boys even at Key Stage 1, with the performance gap widening even further by Key Stage 3. At Key Stage 1 the girls were also ahead in mathematics, but by Key Stage 3 boys' and girls' performance was largely similar. Boys also perform considerably less well than girls in GCSE examinations. It is however dangerous to brand all boys as underachieving, as this is clearly not the case. Their performance, as with that of the girls, is a consequence of interaction with other variables such as social class, ethnic origin and the local context, and for boys in particular, it is the interaction between teacher and pupil in the classroom that makes the biggest impact on achievement.

Social influences when boys are growing up can have an impact on their early learning and performance. Differences become evident in the early years through activities observed in playgroups and nurseries. Girls engage in play activities which they often organise themselves, whereas boys tend to be less structured in their activities and tend to seek the attention of adults. The girls develop the skills aligned to fine motor control earlier than boys, which helps them to be neater, more fluent writers who are better able to deal with the challenges of extended writing than are the boys and thus are better equipped to deal with the demands of school life. By the time they reach secondary schools, for many boys it is more important to be 'one of the lads' than to work hard in school. Schoolwork assumes a low priority compared to socialising and playing sports, and concerns such as homework have little importance.

As has been cited earlier, Learning Mentors can support the boys through focused study support which helps them identify their preferred learning styles, and thus helps with learning and revision for examinations. Assessment methods such as GCSE coursework and continuous assessment have also been shown to discriminate against the boys' preferred ways of working, and support in this area, especially with time management and organisational skills, has proved to be beneficial. Peer group influence is often very negative, and much has been written in the press about the 'laddish culture'. Some Football Association teams, including some from the premier league, have tried to have an influence in this respect and have opened up study support centres in their stadia. Footballers from league teams also work in their local schools at both primary and secondary level helping in PE lessons and after-school clubs. By acting as both role models and motivators to work, the young football stars have undoubtedly made inroads into the boys' attitudes towards work. Tapping in to an interest is often the way forward with many of these youngsters.

A Learning Mentor in Doncaster, writes of her experience with one student:
During his first three years in secondary education Sam was a disruptive influence in class, especially with his peers. He had a violent side, and had been in trouble for 'play fighting'. This had resulted in in-school sanctions, and by the time he was in year 9 he was on the verge of exclusion. Sam attended the Learning Support Centre for six weeks, after which I provided support in mainstream school, had one-to-one mentoring sessions and maintained regular contact with his parents. While working with Sam I established that he had an interest in horses, and indeed he wouldn't engage in productive conversations unless it involved them.

As a way forward we established targets for Sam to improve his behaviour linked to the incentive of visiting a local racing college on its Open Day. His behaviour started to improve and his teachers started to make positive comments about him. He reached his targets and was able to go to the Open Day. He made such a good impression on the visit that in year 10 he will be going to the racing college on a part time basis, and he is no longer at risk of exclusion.

It is, however, important that experiences other than sport, such as music and art, are seen as acceptable to the boys.

Many boys live in a female-dominated culture, especially if when younger they live in a single-mother family, and then attend a female-dominated primary school. Many male role models work in school as volunteer mentors to try to raise the aspirations of the boys and to help them view schools and education more positively. In an effort to raise self-esteem, boys are often encouraged by Learning Mentors to become peer mentors, and to have a higher profile in a range of school activities such as escorting visitors and reception duties.

Of course girls also underachieve and equally are in need of support. Many attend study support sessions, and Learning Mentors have 'girls only' small group sessions to focus on their concerns. Much of their underachievement is linked to insecurity and a fear of looking foolish in front of their peers, low self-esteem and a poor self-image. Some of this is demonstrated in the example below, which describes how a Learning Mentor worked with a female student in Liverpool.

I began working with Claire in her year 9. She was referred to me by her form tutor. Claire was quite a disruptive student who was frequently in trouble, and she appeared to me to be really loud and immature.

I arranged an initial interview with Claire and she was shy and lacking in self-esteem and confidence. I came to believe that she was only loud and disruptive if there was a group of people there to watch. She was an extremely pleasant pupil and realised that she had problems in school. We spoke about the prospect of her joining year 10 and starting her GCSE courses but she was afraid of this. She felt that she had missed too much of her academic work due to exclusions and spells in the Silent Work Area. She did want to improve but was easily led into making other students in her lessons laugh and she did after all have her reputation to maintain.

We met once a week and I monitored her attendance and punctuality, which were fine, the number of detentions she had and the number of times she was sent to the Silent Work Area. There was very little improvement in the beginning. I then asked Claire to join the Mentoring Group which met once each week for circle time and group work. She agreed reluctantly, but after two or three sessions Claire was fine, her outbursts were less frequent and she started focusing on what was positive about her character.

Over time, Claire really began to improve and staff started to notice that she was no longer disruptive in lessons. It was suggested that Claire may be an ideal candidate for a Work Related Curriculum project, and she is now working for two days a week at a hair and beauty salon. Claire says that she now feels a different person and her confidence is at an all-time high. She enjoys coming to school and realises that she can pass some of her GCSE examinations.

Some considerations about ethnic minorities

Much research has been undertaken into the relative achievement of ethnic minority groups, especially with regard to performance at GCSE examinations. Research quoted in Gillborn and Mirza 2000 shows that each of the main ethnic groups now achieve higher attainments at GCSE than ever before, but that African-Caribbean, Pakistani and Bangladeshi pupils are markedly less likely to attain five higher grade GCSEs than their White and Indian peers nationally. The authors further state that the inequalities of attainment for African-Caribbean pupils become progressively greater as they move through the school system; such differences become more pronounced between the end of primary school and the end of secondary school.

The Excellence in Cities initiative operates in many areas which have large concentrations of minority ethnic groups, but the ethnicity of school populations will be unique to particular contexts, and Learning Mentors will need to respond to their own situation. The Government invests funding to support work with minority ethnic pupils (Ethnic Minority Achievement Grant) and this enables specialist teachers and Teaching Assistants to work in schools in support of the pupils and their families. While EMAG-funded staff will be the first line of support for many of these youngsters, it is likely that Learning Mentors will also work with them, in which case collaboration is a must.

Schools that have a culture of achievement are likely to have greatest success with all pupils. High expectations are central to their work, and the provision of intensive support, including that of Learning Mentors, is essential if pupils are to achieve success. Monitoring of pupils' progress, including by ethnicity, enables challenges to be made both regarding staff assumptions and attitudes about pupils' performance and also in relation to the pupils' own perception of their ability. Use of such assessment data is a valuable tool for Learning Mentors in their task of increasing pupils' motivation and aspiration. Volunteer mentors from ethnic minority groups often work in schools. In addition to this, having themselves been successful in the education system, many undergraduates act as mentors in order to raise the aspirations of youngsters in their own communities. These act as positive role models for the youngsters, and have the added advantage of being able to help them with their academic work.

Although white boys experience the highest rates of exclusion, data shows that Black Caribbean and Black African children are disproportionately represented among children who are permanently excluded from school relative to their representation in the whole school population. Many of the exclusions are for fighting or for behaviour which challenges the authority of staff. It is here where conflict often occurs. Ways of communicating and body language can become an issue when, for example, attitudes and stances which the young person finds acceptable are regarded by others as challenging and disrespectful. Because of factors like this, in some cases, Black Caribbean and Black African youngsters and their families feel that their exclusion might have a racial dimension and think that the school does not understand or want to understand. One of the key roles of the Learning Mentor is to find ways of reducing the number of exclusions, and they must be aware of the need for sensitivity and different perspectives when addressing concerns about behaviour.

Much of the work undertaken by a Learning Mentor involves working with the families some of whom are totally unfamiliar with the English schools system, but who value education. Whereas children adjust to the ways of schools and their systems, there is no expectation that this is the case with their families, and ways need to be sought to involve them in their children's education. Familiarising parents, especially the mothers, with the importance of homework, for example, enables them to become involved in their child's education and can contribute in the long term to raising achievement. In some instances, it may be helpful to have information available in community languages, whereas in other cases, making links with the local faith groups through the mosque or temple or making contact with supplementary schools may enable better communication to be established between the school and family. The issue of extended visits abroad, is a contentious one, with schools adopting many different stances towards this.

As a general rule schools dissuade parents from taking their children out of schools for term-time holidays, but when pressed will only give approval for holidays in term time for up to ten days. There are times, however, when families may need to make a trip to visit their extended family abroad, and it is important that schools are sensitive to the different issues involved when making decisions about such visits. A visit to the extended family abroad is an entirely different experience from that normally associated with holiday, and it can bring important educational and cultural benefits to the pupils involved. If Learning Mentors are involved with pupils who undergo such visits they may need to support the pupils in a variety of ways. Before departure they can provide some work for them to do while abroad, and some schools have prepared special study packs for such an event. Perhaps more important is the support the pupils may need when they return to school. It is acknowledged that children who miss school for six weeks may fall behind with their school work by as much as a whole term. This impact will be particularly damaging if the pupils have gone away close to an examination period, whether it be SATs or GCSE examinations. The Learning Mentor can support the pupils through providing a degree of individual help, but also by encouraging attendance at out-of-hours study support sessions and homework clubs. Younger pupils may need help with re-entry problems such as those linked to having to re-establish relationships with other pupils and class teachers.

Some ethnic minority young people have problems with their identities. At school they are members of a Westernised community, while at home they may be part of a close-knit traditional culture. At school they act as typical Western teenagers, doing little to make themselves appear different from their peers, while at home they adopt a role demanded of them by their alternative culture. Many flourish in this situation and take great pride in maintaining the traditions of their communities, but some experience a role conflict and need help coping with their situation. While the Learning Mentor can offer some support, the youngster would be better served by having access to someone who has knowledge of their culture and may have themselves experienced similar difficulties.

Social and economic factors

The ways in which social class and economic status affect educational opportunities are multiple and complex. Some factors lie outside the school, whereas others are consequent on institutional processes which disadvantage certain groups of people. Promotion of self-esteem and increasing aspiration is an important aspect of the work of the Learning Mentor in such circumstances. There is also often a need to compensate for lack of interest at home. Some pupils are in effect both bringing themselves up and having responsibility for siblings. Little interest is shown in their education by parents who themselves gave up on education at the earliest opportunity. Some parents work irregular hours and can only do so as long as the children organise themselves. Learning Mentors need to be aware of the home context if they are to offer effective support.

Some of the issues are implicit in this description by a Learning Mentor of the neighbourhood around a primary and secondary school on an outer city council estate. Despite massive problems, the Learning Mentor remained optimistic that she and the other mentors were starting to make a difference.

> Although there are many positive and aspirational families on the estate we tend not to have much to do with them as their children on the whole are coping well in school.
>
> Many other families have lived on the estate for over twenty years and themselves attended the local schools. Their own experience of school was negative and they cannot believe that the schools have changed; they certainly have not visited the schools to find out. The community therefore has a negative impression of their local schools and is unwilling to work with them in support of their children.
>
> The schools are made the scapegoat for some of the poor behaviour of the children and this deflects responsibility away from the parents. Parents become aggressive and defensive when approached by the school, even if the reasons for contact are positive.
>
> Many of the parents have low educational standards and no history of employment, so they feel that academic qualifications are irrelevant. Children receive little support from home. Many of the families are on the lowest income or income support and are dependent on benefits. Education spending for them will be a low priority.

The Learning Mentors have to challenge the pupils' low opinion of themselves, and their feeling of self-worth. They have to compensate for possible lack of support at home by ensuring that the support is freely given at school. Their self-esteem is influenced by what they think others, including their parents, think of them, and so raising self-esteem has to be a priority. By having time alone with the Learning Mentor the pupils can start to feel special and valued. Being praised at school for their individual achievement makes them feel successful, and this further gives them confidence to learn new skills. The process of target-setting with the Learning Mentor enables such praise to be given in a private environment. Homework will present particular difficulties for pupils from homes where there is little physical space where the pupil can work, and little willingness to give them the time and peace to undertake any schoolwork. Lunchtime and after-school homework clubs can compensate to some extent, and Learning Mentors often target particular pupils to attend these. Breakfast clubs have the additional advantage of ensuring that the child has something to eat at the start of the day.

Financial concerns give rise to difficulties, some of which the Learning Mentor can help with. By working with families, they can ensure that the families receive all of the educational financial benefits to which they are entitled. In many cases this will mean access to free dinners, and in some instances, help with grants for uniforms. In one authority, which did not give uniform grants, the Learning Mentor was able to access funds through a local community organisation which offered to help purchase uniforms for the most needy, as long as they lived on the estate served by the group. Money for other school activities such as trips and PE equipment will not be a priority, and again the Learning Mentor may need to talk to teachers on behalf of the children to explain their situation. Certainly these pupils will not be wearing the latest designer trainers and may be victims of pupil taunts because of this.

Some families in such areas are second and third-generation unemployed, and unless some type of intervention occurs, the children will have no aspiration about any future employment for themselves. In such circumstances, certainly an exhortation to achieve academic success in order to 'get a good job' will have little impact on either the pupil or the family. A few families may use 'non-mainstream' methods of making money which provide financial gain for relatively little effort. Such apathy has been countered by some Learning Mentors who have invited successful members of the local community, including past pupils, to come into school and share their experiences with the disaffected youngsters. This could lead to group discussion where the group are encouraged to review their stance and hopefully, with support, to work towards developing a more positive outlook. Intervention by a Personal Adviser may also be beneficial as they would have knowledge of work and training availability in the area.

An inclusive school

An inclusive school is one which truly meets the needs of the community it serves, and through developing flexible ways of working is able to support the educational needs of all children in the local community. Such a school would endeavour to provide each pupil with whatever support they may need to overcome barriers to learning. Learning Mentors work at the interface between the school and the community and can be instrumental, with the support of others in the school, in gaining support for the school within the community, often by working with some of the more 'difficult' but influential families. Figure 6.3 summarises some of the elements of an inclusive school which impact on the work of a Learning Mentor to a greater or lesser degree.

Parents and other members of the community should feel welcome as soon as they enter the school. If a Learning Mentor is expecting a visitor they should inform the receptionist of this so that when the visitors arrive they can be greeted by name and made to feel welcome. The school should ideally have signs which use symbols as well as texts in all the community languages, and this practice should extend to the

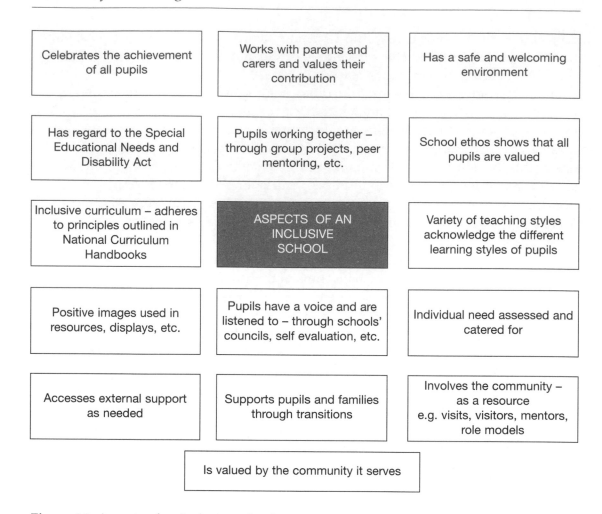

Figure 6.3 Aspects of an inclusive school

Learning Mentor's room. Many Learning Mentors have adopted the habit of having a range of toys in their room and personalising them in various ways, both to help children who are upset, and also in acknowledgement of the fact that some of the parents who visit them will have to bring younger children with them.

All pupils should be aware that their work is valued. Their work should be displayed, not always that which is perfect, but also some less than perfect work which nevertheless reflects a pupil's best effort. Such work can also be a useful stimulus for discussion between a Learning Mentor and pupil as the pupil is asked to consider what enabled them to perform at such a high level in that particular instance. Learning Mentors frequently take part in assemblies, especially those which celebrate success, and write 'good news' letters to parents outlining the successes of their children. As a means of promoting the youngsters' self-esteem, Learning Mentors are often to be found working with the children on talent shows, community celebrations and special projects which enable them to demonstrate their ability and form a point of contact with the community. Working with community musicians, 'artists in residence' or a local photographer have enabled youngsters to gain a deeper insight into their communities while developing special talents of their own.

In a truly inclusive school pupils have the opportunity to express opinions and know that they are being listened to. Much of the small group work and circle time activities undertaken by Learning Mentors gives the pupils the confidence to speak out. School councils are the commonest example of pupil empowerment, and Learning Mentors regularly support pupils with these, but the councils can only be successful if they are allowed to discuss real issues of concern to them, and notice is taken of the outcomes of their debate. Especially valuable are opportunities where pupils have input into decisions about school policies, particular those relating to behaviour and discipline. The Learning Mentor has a real advantage over other adults working in the school in this respect as they are able to give time to listen to individuals.

The community is a valuable resource. There are a wealth of people and organisations who are very willing to work with the school. In particular, businesses and services may offer work experience places to pupils, or offer staff to act as mentors or role models within the school. Libraries are a major resource, offering access to a wealth of information as well as running excellent homework and study support clubs. For those who wish to develop their Internet skills but do not have easy access to a computer, these are often available in the local library. Learning Mentors are often involved in multi-agency initiatives in the community working with the Education Welfare Service, Police, Social Services and the Health Service.

Finally, in considering the inclusive environment of the school and beyond, Learning Mentors may well find the 'index for inclusion' (CSIE) to be of help. As it sets out in its summary:

> The *index* is a set of materials to support schools in a process of inclusive development. It is about building supportive school communities which foster high achievement for all students.

If mentors take time to consider this useful resource it will most certainly give 'food for thought' and may well provide a number of ideas and resources.

7 Monitoring and evaluation

Schools of today are now very familiar with the process of monitoring and evaluation and, in turn, its value in providing information for future planning. It is a process that is in the interests of the whole school. Achieving a continuous cycle of improvement can only be of benefit to all, and as a part of the school, the Learning Mentor should see themselves as having a very important role to play in all of this.

The need to prove effectiveness

As we have seen, the role of the Learning Mentor is to work with individual children with the aim of enabling them to re-engage in the learning process. There is a need, however, in the current educational climate for the Learning Mentor to be aware of the need to provide evidence of their effectiveness. How can you prove that you have made a difference? What evidence do you have that can demonstrate that you have had impact upon, for example, the reduction in exclusions in your school or the increase in attendance percentages? It is quite easy to say –'I know I have made a difference,' but proving it is a different matter. To establish effectiveness, with a good evidence base that is open to scrutiny, may seem to be a frightening prospect; but take heart, we can assure you that mentors probably have a multitude of evidence available at their fingertips. Let us start by taking a closer look at the work that is the focal point of the Learning Mentor.

Working with individual pupils

Figure 7.1 provides a basic, generic outline of a possible working system based on a six-week cycle (although mentors may not work in exactly the same way, we would suggest that something similar might well be in place). Working through such a process brings with it the automatic need for providing and requesting information, and for recording and reporting outcomes. The paperwork required to do this is a huge evidence base, and the Learning Mentor would do well to consider that whatever they have designed, it should:

- be aimed at meeting the needs of the child in the first instance but, at the same time, provide information for monitoring and evaluation purposes;
- be as short and succinct as possible. Regardless of whether it is adults or children who are being asked to complete it, they will be most reluctant if faced with a seemingly endless list of questions (incomplete or missing paperwork is not going to provide good evidence!).

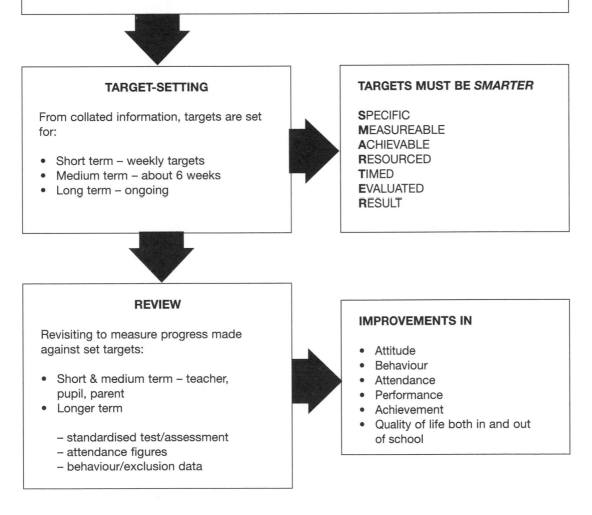

Figure 7.1 Outline for a working system of monitoring and evaluation

If we start by looking at the work of the mentor with an individual pupil as outlined in 7.1, from entry to exit, we can perhaps examine the range of information required to support them throughout. Figure 7.2 outlines a structure that may form the basis of the process, and within it there is an obvious opportunity to develop paperwork that will not only support the child but in turn support the work of the mentor in their efforts to monitor and evaluate.

If we take each section in turn it will allow consideration of how the mentor may in fact develop a system of recording and reporting.

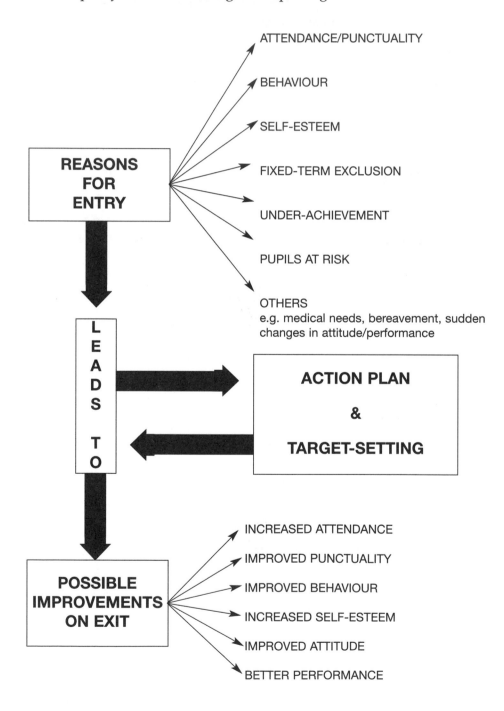

Figure 7.2 Outline structure for mentoring process

Reasons for entry

At the point of entry, the child will have been referred because of a concern that has been identified by one or more of the following:

- teacher(s), through
    - subject staff who have concerns within their own subject area
    - pastoral staff who have an overview of the child who is causing concern
    - a combination of both
- parent(s)/carer(s)
- SENCO
- the child (self-referral)
- a friend of a pupil
- EWS

Whatever the point of referral, this needs to be recorded, and at that point an overall profile formulated to provide as much information about the child as is possible. This will require a gathering of evidence that might involve pre-designed forms or personal interviews with the child, parents, teachers and the child's friends to establish an overall picture. In addition, there will be the statistical information on factors such as, for example, test/examination scores, recorded predicted grades, and attendance figures. Mentors have a multitude of ways in which they gather and record such information, and while researching the book, we have been privileged to see a wide range. It would, however, be impractical for us to provide sufficient examples that would do justice to the good work being done, and therefore we would like to offer a profile sheet for consideration. Figure 7.3 is based around the areas listed in Figure 7.2 at the entry level and examples of paperwork currently in use by mentors.

Initially the sheet gives a readily available picture of the reason for the child's referral, but it also collates a range of information on one sheet that is easily transferable when trying to collate information for specific purposes of recording and reporting to a wider audience. For example, the total number of children referred to the mentor due to exclusions or those referred due to poor attendance. If mentors take time to examine the profile sheet it may allow them time to reflect and establish whether they have sufficient systems in place that would allow them to readily transfer such information on one sheet. It may in the long term make their lives much easier when information is required for evaluation purposes.

Action plan and target-setting

Once the initial referral has taken place the Learning Mentor is into the process of action-planning and target-setting. It is here where most of the information gleaned will be from one-to-one discussions with the pupil. We would suggest that the main points to consider when devising the paperwork should be:

- Targets to be achieved (these may be set on short, medium and long-term basis)
- Strategies for achieving the targets (including support systems and special arrangements)

ENTRY RECORD

Name of pupil: _____ **Attendance:** Last 6 weeks _____%

Previous Term _____%

D.O.B. __ / __ / __   **Class:** _____   **Ethnicity:** _____

Referred by: Subject/Class Teacher ☐   Tutor/Head of Year ☐

Self-referral ☐   Other child/Friend ☐   Parent/Carer ☐

EWS ☐   Other referral ☐   Details: _____

Reason for referral: Attendance ☐   Attitude ☐

Behaviour ☐   Low Self-esteem ☐   Under-performance ☐

Exclusion ☐   Other ☐   Details: _____

Positive Comments

Main areas of concern:

Action points:

Date _____

Figure 7.3 Profile sheet

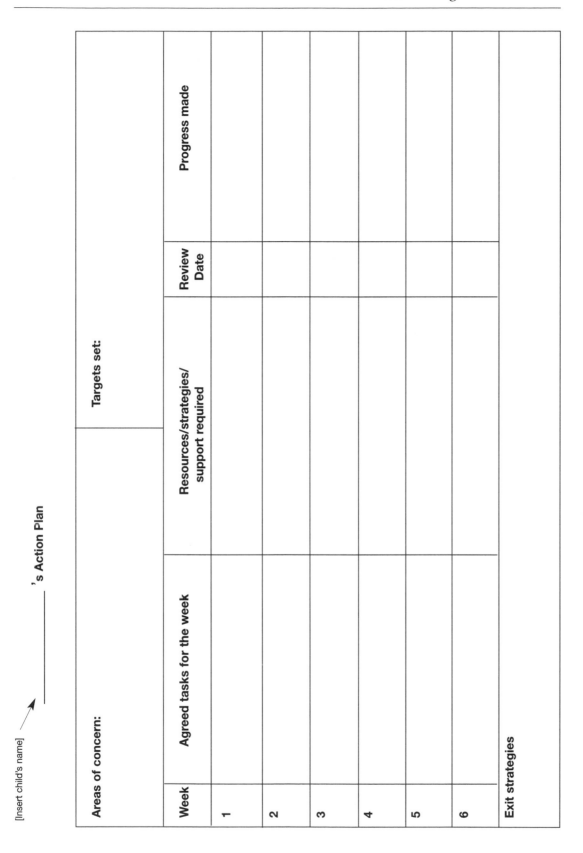

Figure 7.4 Action plan form

- Timescales for the targets
- Criteria for achieving the targets including Exit Criteria
- Approximate deadlines for completion

Completing the paperwork is best done with the child as they will feel fully involved in the whole process, feel ownership towards it and be more likely to make a greater effort towards achieving the set targets. Once again there is a plethora of examples in use within schools, and Figure 7.4 has been designed by taking account of some in current use in a number of schools.

Exiting the programme

At the point of exit from the programme of intervention by the mentor, the paperwork required will need to record the results of the whole process, stating improvements made in targeted areas, and taking into account once again any appropriate data, and feedback from all interested parties. Learning Mentors have a range of forms for providing feedback, but consideration should be given to those who may prefer to give feedback in verbal rather than in written form. It would once again be an advantage to the Learning Mentor if they had a master sheet to collate all of the feedback, which would give an immediate picture of how successful their intervention had been. Figure 7.5 is an example of what may serve such a purpose. It allows for quick analysis of a number of points that may be needed for recording and reporting purposes but more importantly it gives an overview of how and where the mentor's intervention has had impact.

Looking at the whole process of the work of the Learning Mentors from entry to exit and the recording and reporting that takes place throughout enables us to appreciate the range and depth of information available. There will in addition to this be the work of the mentor with those children who are involved with group sessions rather than individual work.

Working with groups

Some group work will in fact be organised to deal with the needs of individual pupils, such as, for example, circle time and anger management, where work is required on aspects such as self-esteem and emotional literacy. Where this is the case, the impact will still remain part of the pupil's individual evaluation and be evaluated accordingly.

Other group work taking place in schools that may be organised by the Learning Mentor concerns a larger number of pupils and is often focused around out-of-hours learning. These sessions work towards enabling pupils to deal with the demands that education places upon them, to help them to develop their abilities in coping with a range of internal and external pressures, and to help them build their confidence and self-esteem. We would suggest that in these instances, it would be unrealistic to expect a mentor to record and report on each individual's progress. It is, however, still important to be able to measure impact, and we must therefore

EXIT RECORD

Name of pupil: _____ **D.O.B.** _ / _ / _   **Class:** _____

Ethnicity: _____ **Attendance:** Last 6 weeks _____%

Feedback recieved from:

                   Subject/Class Teacher ☐   Tutor/Head of Year ☐

Pupil ☐   Other child/Friend ☐   Parent/Carer ☐

EWS ☐   Other ☐   Details: _____

Improvements recorded in:

Attendance ☐   Attitude ☐   Behaviour ☐

Self Esteem ☐   Performance ☐

Other ☐   Details: _____

Positive Comments on areas of improvement:

Longer term action points:

Date _____

Figure 7.5 Summary sheet

PERRY BEECHES SCHOOL
STUDENT SUPPORT PROGRAMME
ANALYSIS OF MENTORING SUPPORT

One to one support

Year Group	Total	Gender		FSM	EAL	SEN	Ethnicity			
		G	B				W	AC	A	MR
7	3	1	2				1	1		1
8	5	1	4					5		
9	11	3	8				2	5		4
10	10	3	7				3	7		
11	12	2	10				5	6		1
Totals	41	10	31				11	24		6
%	100	24	76				27	58	0	15
School Total %	100	53	47	28	28	30	46	16	26	0

There is a large over representation of boys;: African–Caribbean students; Mixed Race students and an under-representation of Asian and White students.

Year 11 Academic 1:1/Group Mentoring Support Programme

Total No. of Students	60	%	School %
Boys	29	48	53
Girls	31	52	47
SEN			
EAL			
Ethnicity			
White	27	45	46
African–Caribbean	13	22	16
Asian	17	28	26
Mixed Race	3	5	0

There is a slight over reprensentation of girls referred to academic support. Ethnicity is relatively in line with school figures

Group Support

Year group 7, 8, 9 10 and 11	Total No of Students	Gender		Ethnicity			
		M	F	White	African-Caribbean	Asian	Mixed Race
Behaviour Management	10	10		4	6		
Social Skills	19	13	6	7	10		2
Assertiveness Training	4	1	3	3			1
Anger Management	12	10	2	4	5	2	1
Totals	45	34	11	18	21	2	4
%	100	76	24	40	47	4	9
School %	100	53	47	46	16	26	0

•There is a large over-representation of boys; African-Caribbean students and an under-representation of mixed race students.

• There is a large under-representation of girls and Asian students.

Figure 7.6 Perry Beeches School analysis of support

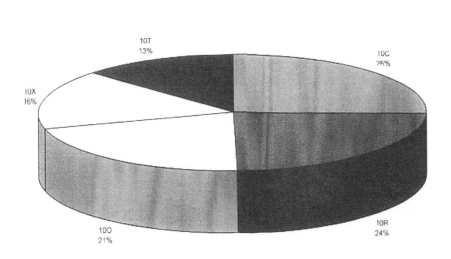

Participation Rates in Study Support Activities
2001-2002, Year 10.

Figure 7.7 Croxteth Community Comphrehensive School participation rates

consider how this can be achieved. To evaluate effectively, there has to be a two-pronged approach that takes into account short-term and longer-term evaluation.

Short-term impact should be measured by the uptake by pupils, their continued attendance over a period of time and, perhaps, the consideration of the overall impact upon their confidence and self-esteem during a set period of time. In addition to this, it may be that specific questions are asked about identified groups, for example, participation of ethnic groups. Examples of some of this type of record-keeping and evaluation can be seen in Figures 7.6 and 7.7, where the Learning Mentors have collated information for specific purposes in respect of attendance at group sessions.

The longer-term impact focuses more on use of data from external sources and should measure progress against predetermined criteria, for example, actual grades/scores against predicted grades/scores. This is where the mentor, as part of the pupil's baseline assessment, will have gathered information at the outset from standardised tests/assessments or teacher predictions. On receiving the results from external tests/exams, comparisons can be made to evaluate against the original baselines whether any significant impact has been made. This can be done for individuals and groups. In relation to groups, it could also enable the mentor to demonstrate their impact on an identified cohort, such as:

- Boys or girls
- Identified ethnic groups

- Vulnerable children – for example, children in care, young carers
- Gifted and Talented
- Pupils at risk of exclusion

Working with others

The Learning Mentor will also be involved in other work that involves a wider community than that of the pupils within the school. This may well involve work with any number of the following:

- Local community
- Parents
- Cross-phase
- Link mentors
- Gifted and Talented co-ordinators
- Volunteer mentors
- Community groups

Once again, the mentor needs to consider how to report and record such work. We would suggest this does not require laborious lengthy reports. A note of statistical information on involvement alongside a brief synopsis of outcomes of this type of work will suffice, but it could include minutes of meetings. It will often be additional to the main focus of working with the children; however, it is none the less important and can be used alongside the evidence gathered from working with individuals and groups to provide a range of information for monitoring and evaluation purposes.

Monitoring and evaluation

Monitoring and evaluation of practice is a vital part of the Learning Mentor's work. It is the way in which evidence of effective working can be gathered and used to demonstrate the impact of their practice. It may well be required by a number of different audiences, which may include:

- School – teachers, middle management, senior management, Headteacher, governors
- LEA – link mentor, school improvement teams, Excellence in Cities, Education Action Zones
- Ofsted
- HMI

So, how should the Learning Mentor go about developing a system that will provide relevant information and suit a range of audiences? To answer this question, there is a need first to consider what monitoring and evaluation is all about.

Establishing the purpose

Monitoring and Evaluation is about the gathering, collation and consideration of information for a predetermined purpose. The results of such a process are aimed at providing evidence of success and effectiveness with regard to preset criteria. There is also a need to recognise where criteria are not met, there is a need for change.

How to do it

Monitoring and evaluation needs to be productive, otherwise it serves no purpose and simply becomes a paper exercise with no reward for all of those involved. Before panic sets in, Learning Mentors should take time to look at the paperwork, processes and systems they already have in place. As we have seen through this chapter, there are numerous opportunities for recording information, so the most important thing to ensure is that whatever is there, it provides sufficient evidence to enable an evaluation of effectiveness.

There are a number of ways in which we can monitor and gather evidence but we would suggest that the starting point should be to establish the purpose behind the action. Figure 7.8 sets out a series of questions that may assist in the process of monitoring and evaluation. By going through them in order it may help to determine:

- whether what is being monitored is of relevance and of importance;
- whether there is enough readily available evidence, or
- whether there is a need to 'custom design' to meet pre-set criteria

The most important factors are providing for the gathering of evidence and the evaluation of the evidence in respect of the impact and effectiveness of the Learning Mentor's work.

What to do with the results?

Once the process has been completed, the Learning Mentor will have evidence of what has proved to be effective and what may need to be changed. This can then be used for reporting purposes to the predetermined audience(s). Common practice is to keep a portfolio of sample evidence in a ring binder.

Learning Mentors may also wish to take the opportunity at this point to formulate a development plan, in which possible or future changes can be identified. This will allow for predetermining what needs to be done, how it is going to be done and whether there are any costs to be incurred at any point. Schools continually plan through whole school, departmental and individual plans, and it may indeed help the Learning Mentor to be a part of this system. Figure 7.9 provides an example of a common type of proforma that may be of use.

Having looked at the monitoring and evaluation of practice, the associated paperwork for recording and reporting, and the future planning to be considered, let us now move on to look at the range of work that is being done by mentors in a number of schools.

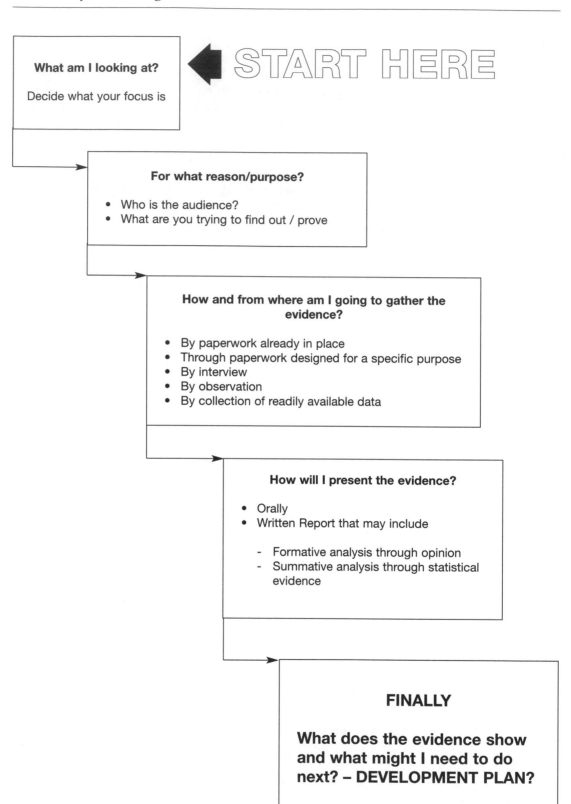

Figure 7.8 Understanding monitoring and evaluation

LEARNING MENTOR DEVELOPMENT PLAN

Action to be taken	How and by who	Date for completion	Monitored by:	Criteria for success	Resources e.g inset, funding, time, materials

Figure 7.9 Sample development plan

8 The reality

In this chapter we are going to consider the diverse role of the Learning Mentor, particularly at crucial stages and transitions in the pupil's school experience. It uses examples of good practice, and demonstrates that although Learning Mentors may have a common title, the role is open to wide interpretation dependent on the nature of and needs of the school.

The infant school

A successful entry to infant school lays the foundation for a successful school career, and therefore it is in the interest of the school to make the place as welcoming and supportive as possible. In this, many infant schools excel, and they present themselves as vibrant learning centres totally open to and part of the local community. Parents need to feel that they can entrust their children to the school, and to some degree reassuring them is as important as looking after the children.

Isabella Ellis is a Learning Mentor in Wilkes Green Infant School in Handsworth, Birmingham. She is a graduate with vast experience of working in schools and the community in a variety of roles, and is currently undertaking a Master's degree in multicultural education. She is based in a room which she and the pupils call 'the cell' but which is in reality a cheerful, welcoming room with bright yellow walls centrally located in the school.

Isabella's philosophy is one of sharing and caring, and she uses the slogan 'United in Education' as her logo. She wants everyone to achieve the best they can and works unstintingly to make this happen. Her mentees include parents as well as the children, on the basis that the parents have to be happy if the children are to be happy. Although formal mentoring times with individual pupils and small groups is sacrosanct, Isabella is available to support parents, pupils and teachers as needed. This is no 9.00 am to 3.30 pm job, and Isabella has two mobile phones, one of which is used exclusively for work – the number is given to those who may need to contact her out of school hours.

Meeting the needs

The pupils' needs are many and varied and Isabella works with them on a one-to-one basis, in small groups, or gives them support in class. Many of the pupils are learning English as a second language and some need additional help with integrating successfully in the classroom. Because they cannot yet understand what the teachers or other pupils are saying, they start to exhibit poor behaviour and need help over and above that given by bilingual assistants. Pupils with low self-esteem get help with motivation and the development of a more positive self-image. Some children are very bright, but have poorly developed communication skills and are afraid to speak. They play games such as Chinese Whispers, or, by prior arrangement, are sent to take a message to the office, which forces them to speak to the staff. Some of the six-year olds, quite understandably, become distressed at the thought of the Key Stage 1 SATs examinations and they are given extra help with literacy and numeracy or with the personal skills needed to help them better cope with the assessments. Parental consent is always obtained before formal mentoring takes place. Isabella is herself multilingual and this is a real asset in a school where so many languages are spoken. The diversity of language is celebrated and pupils quickly learn to communicate with one another in a variety of ways until the basics of English are learnt.

Recognising achievement

Many opportunities are given to recognise the achievement of the pupils. On Friday afternoon Isabella has a 'Thumbs Up' group which is for children who have done consistently well during the week. Pupils who have excellent attendance receive certificates and rewards, and badges are given for punctuality as part of the 'Early Bird' scheme. The children's work is displayed everywhere, and photographs remind them of participation in a range of events.

Dealing with attendance

Isabella works closely with the Education Welfare Officer on matters relating to attendance. Prior to making home visits, she rings the parent to introduce herself and explain the reason for the visit and is always welcomed. Extended visits abroad are usually planned well in advance and work is provided for the child. Support with reintegration is provided on the child's return should it be needed. An expected date of return is agreed with the school, and parents are warned that this must be strictly adhered to. So effective is this that it has resulted in phone calls being received for example from India when a domestic crisis has forced the visit to be extended, and from Jamaica when a family's return was delayed by a hurricane.

Moving on

Children have to be supported with their transition from the infant school to the junior school, and although in this school it involves movement to another part of

101

the same site, it nevertheless produces major psychological barriers in the minds of some children. Isabella involves them in a programme of role-play in which they can work through some of the anticipated issues, and circle time/nurture groups where concerns are further discussed. Practical help is also given. This is also a time of change for parents who have to start developing relationships with a new group of staff and Isabella is mindful of offering support to them too.

Parent partnership

Under the guidance of Isabella, the school has a strong Parent Partnership programme. Projects which the parents can join include: aromatherapy, mehndi, nail- painting, computers, English as a second language, and self-defence. Some parents now have the confidence to help in the school and are learning to be Classroom Assistants. Coffee mornings are held, at which parents can informally meet the teachers, and hopefully this will allay their fears of teachers as 'authority figures', based on their own past experience of school. Despite their apparent approachability, teachers still manage to confuse parents by their use of language and jargon, and some parents will go to Isabella and give her a verbatim account of a conversation with a teacher and ask her to tell them what the conversation was actually about. She will similarly help parents to fill in official forms and accompany them to a range of appointments, such as a visit to the doctor, where they do not feel confident of understanding what is going on.

Linking with the community

Close links are maintained with the community, both formally and informally. The local fire station provides much support, as does a local organisation which attempts to provide training which will re-engage adults in education and work. The school is fully involved in community projects such as celebrating Marcus Garvey Day in the local park, and having a Jubilee party in the school. Isabella accesses help for the children from local mentoring, arts and business groups such as The Voices of Ujima, who provide mentoring through music, art and dance.

Mentees and their parents stay in contact long after the children have left the school, a tribute to the confidence and trust that Isabella has managed to instil in them. She is keen to share good practice and has her own website which allows mentors worldwide to exchange ideas.

The primary school

One of the most immediate things that strikes any visitor to Deykin Avenue Junior and Infant School in Birmingham is the strong sense of community, where every individual is genuinely valued and cared about. The walls are covered with displays showing off the work and achievements of the pupils, and the Learning Mentor's room is similarly covered with the work of children, including the many letters that they have sent to Denise Fox the Learning Mentor.

Denise brings a wealth of experience to her role as a primary Learning Mentor, having already worked as a secondary Learning Mentor, a support worker in a Pupil Referral Unit and as a policewoman. She is also a qualified teacher of meditation and head massage, and these therapeutic qualities form an innovative focus for her work.

The Diversity of the work

One of the greatest skills of the Learning Mentor is the ability to be flexible and to prioritise need. Although Denise has regular commitments to classes and individuals during the week, there are times when she just has to respond to an urgent concern. She may need to drop everything to comfort and support a year 1 child whose dog has been run over; or someone's gran has died and they have been reminded of it in a story they have just read and they have broken down. Alternatively, one of the mentees may be having a bad time in a lesson and has thrown a wobbly, deciding that school is not for him, and needs help.

Dealing with diversity

Denise has introduced many practical ideas, some with the help of her husband's woodworking skills. In the school hall stands a bright red Worry Box into which children can post their concerns. She has a Feelings Tree with hand crafted wooden fruit inscribed with emotions such as worry, fear, happiness, sadness and grief which is used as a resource in assemblies and circle time. A bright yellow Positive Thoughts Box allows children to share good ideas, and a bright yellow mirror with words inscribed on it to raise self-esteem allows everyone to look into the mirror and see something positive. Children regularly use smaller mirrors to help focus on self-esteem; they are urged to look into the mirror and talk about what they see. At first only a few were able to talk about what they could see, but with regular use of the technique Denise finds that when she undertakes this exercise with the children she is bombarded with responses from the youngsters who want to talk about the goodness they see inside their hearts. One of the biggest successes is the 'Cool to be Kind' awards which are two wooden smiling faces inscribed with 'It's cool to be kind' and these are given out in a Merit Assembly to Key Stage 1 and Key Stage 2 children who deserve them. She also offers music and drama clubs for the pupils and runs a School Council.

Denise works with children who have anger and self-esteem difficulties. She uses the traffic light system to help the children reflect on their behaviour – stop means calm down and think about the problem, wait means think about how you are feeling, and go means think about what you need to do. Children in trouble are now used to thinking through aspects of their behaviour and coming to a conclusion themselves about what they need to do to resolve the problem. Anger management is very friendly and informal and revolves around the use of a red and black anger bag, made by Denise's daughter. The bag, filled with polystyrene balls, is passed around the group and when it is a child's turn to talk they can punch the bag as hard as they like as they describe what has made them angry.

The introduction of meditation into the school is another innovative aspect of Denise's work and one that really has made a difference. Meditation is regularly used in the school both in classrooms and in assembly and all the children have had the chance to learn the skill. It takes six minutes, and Denise talks the children through the process. They do breathing and relaxation techniques. She then talks them through visualisation where they go to their special place which is private and personal to them. They then sit completely still, listen to the music for 2–3 minutes, dismiss any thoughts that come into their heads, and just focus on their body being relaxed. There have been many positive benefits and the children look forward to their meditation sessions. The classrooms have become calmer learning environments, where pupils are more focused on their work, and the playground has become more peaceful with fewer conflicts taking place. Some examples of the children's responses to meditation are shown in Figure 8.1.

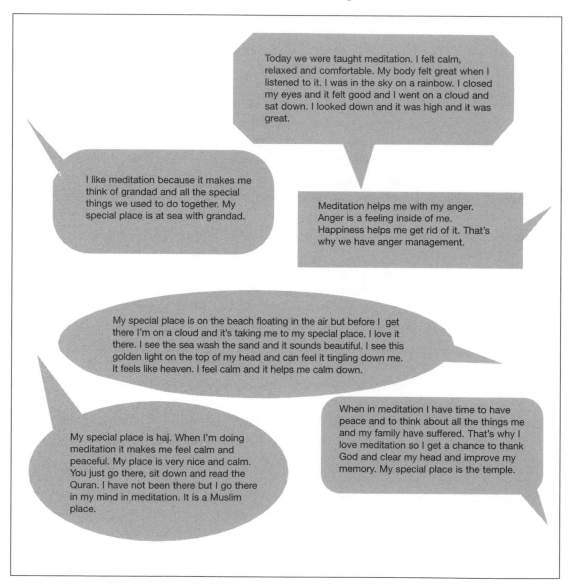

Figure 8.1 Children's reflections on meditation

Working with parents and teachers

One of the most fulfilling aspects of Denise's role is working with parents. However friendly a school is, it can still be a daunting place for parents, and so Denise often visits parents at home. Children from many different cultures attend the school, and it certainly helps parents to meet on their own territory. She recently visited a family where their child had been knocked over by a car going the wrong way down their street. She took the girl a large card made by her class telling her that they loved her and missed her and looked forward to her return. Denise sees support for teachers as part of her role and undertakes in-class support as needed. She co-ordinates circle time and PSHE for the school and meets each class weekly. She has also organised a Holistic Therapy Day for the staff when they were able to experience for themselves the benefits of aromatherapy body massage, Indian head massage, reflexology and meditation.

In conclusion, Denise sums up her role as: 'The job of a mentor meets lots of criteria and each position is unique and individual. A lot of the job is what you make of it. It's hard, time consuming, it's rewarding and stimulating. I find it a privilege that these children let me into their minds and share with me their innermost thoughts and feelings. It's wonderful, and the best job I'll ever do.'

Cross-phase support: primary to secondary schools

Moving from primary to secondary school can be both exciting and a traumatic time for children, and indeed a few get totally lost to the formal education system at this stage. Parents also have different reactions. Those that are confident embrace the challenge with enthusiasm, while those who were themselves not particularly successful at school often find the whole notion intimidating and thus find it hard to give their child the support s/he needs at this stage.

Learning Mentors have a specific remit with regard to cross-phase transfer which is to promote speedy and effective transfer of pupil information from primary to secondary schools in order to smooth transition. Most also liaise between the schools in order to identify vulnerable youngsters.

Learning Mentors who work in primary schools establish links with the secondary schools, especially liaising with the Learning Mentors, while secondary Learning Mentors, as part of a whole school process, establish links with the primary school and a programme of getting to know one another's children and routines becomes established. The mentors will work in partnership with other school staff, including possibly the year 6 teachers, Head of year 7 and the Special Needs and Inclusion Co-ordinators. Learning Mentors may attend open days and year 6 and 7 parents' evenings at both schools and thus offer continuity of support to pupils and their parents.

Some parents will need a great deal of support throughout the whole transfer process and primary Learning Mentors are well placed to provide this. The choice of school can be relatively simple if traditionally most children go to the same secondary school. Where a choice of secondary school exists, children and parents will be faced with invitations to open days, induction days, etc. The confident parent will enjoy this and go everywhere, taking pride in asking challenging questions of the headteacher, while others, probably the majority, will find the whole process daunting and leave it up to the child to decide. Parents do, however, have paperwork to complete and deadlines to meet, and the primary Learning Mentor can be very supportive and help the parents through the whole transfer process.

Getting to know the children who are transferring becomes an important part of the work of the secondary Learning Mentor, while the primary Learning Mentors seek to familiarise themselves with the routines of the secondary school in order to better serve their year 6 pupils. Learning Mentors from both phases undertake work with year 6 pupils and in some instances get involved in joint year 6 and year 7 projects of both a curricular and social nature. Typical of this is the secondary Learning Mentor who took year 7 pupils to a local primary school after school, and undertook coaching of year 6 football and netball teams. When the year 6 pupils transferred to the secondary school, the pupils not only knew some older pupils in the school, but the school had ready-made year 7 sports teams!

Use of peer mentors is a growth area in respect of pupil transfer, and many Learning Mentors are responsible for their training and supervision. Learning Mentors will themselves require training before they can effectively undertake this work, and an example of such training is given in Chapter 9. Schools typically apply their own criteria for the selection of peer mentors, and these may not be the pupils who are already known to the Learning Mentor. Pupils selected as peer mentors may be in year 9 and start to work intensively in primary schools once they have completed their SATs examinations. They will have some preliminary training concerned with, for example, how to talk to children, active listening skills, the importance of confidentiality, engaging pupils in play which would promote personal/social skills, and issues that are likely to worry the children who are about to transfer. Examples of peer mentors' involvement in primary–secondary transfer include:

Pre-transfer
- working with year 6 pupils in primary schools
- showing year 6 pupils around the secondary school
- attending parents' evenings which are held as part of the transfer process
- taking part in induction programmes
- accompanying year 6 primary school children on a residential visit
- taking part in joint sport/music activities
- writing and publishing a pupil information booklet about the school.

Post-transfer
- acting as 'buddies' to pupils who were known to be vulnerable
- visiting year 7 tutorial sessions
- supporting year 7 pupils on a one-to-one basis
- holding 'drop-in' sessions for year 7 pupils where they can help to resolve problems, help with school work and develop personal and social skills.

Peer mentoring schemes are mutually beneficial to both parties, but the pupil mentors themselves need to understand the boundaries of their relationship, and their activities need to be carefully supervised and monitored by the Learning Mentor. The new year 7 pupils receive support at a crucial time in their lives. They make new friends and have someone to talk to who will help them with schoolwork or personal problems. They also learn to interact with others and develop a range of personal and social skills. These are all skills which the Learning Mentor can reinforce if necessary.

Some secondary schools have found that cross-phase peer mentoring programmes and Learning Mentor support, because of their involvement with primary schools, have positively increased the profile of the school in the community, and this has resulted in improved recruitment and an increase in pupil numbers. Such a programme is also able to enhance existing pastoral provision and acknowledges that some children find it easier to talk to other children than adults.

It is also acknowledged that many pupils appear to regress during the transition from primary to secondary school, and such regression will be greater for those who lack the social competence to cope with the transfer. Learning Mentors are able to work with pupils in both years 6 and 7 to help them cope with their anticipated worries. Much of this work involves allaying their fears, and sometimes the fears of their parents and may involve taking a child and his parents or a small group to visit the secondary school in addition to the standard visits arranged for the whole year group. Many of the children's fears can be quickly dismissed, but none should be ignored, as small problems may for some children assume enormous proportions unless they are dealt with effectively.

Common concerns include:

- not being able to afford a new uniform
- getting used to a longer journey to school
- having to relate to a large number of new teachers
- lack of friends or being lonely
- having nothing to do at breaks/lunchtimes
- homework
- work which is too hard
- not feeling safe in a large school
- being the youngest
- being bullied, having head put down the toilet
- getting in trouble, detentions
- being away from home for a long time
- lack of interest or support from other family members.

Many children will quickly resolve these problems for themselves, but the Learning Mentor may have to offer extra support to others.

Summer schools are held in many schools, and whereas some of these are part of the Key Stage 3 strategy to raise standards and thus focus on literacy and numeracy, others are promoted as developing personal social skills or even just having fun!

Table 8.1

Nature of referral	Activity	Measure of Success
Anxiety about transfer	One-to-one mentoring was undertaken twice a week during June and July. The pupils gained in confidence during a potentially very stressful period.	Pupils looking forward to the transfer. They know that their mentor will be supporting them when they get to Kings Norton High School.
Erratic attenders	Two pupils had erratic attendance and regular lateness during Autumn and Spring Terms of year 6. Mentor worked with the pupils on the importance of attending regularly and being on time at the secondary school. Praise given every day that they attended and rewarded when they had been on time every day for two weeks.	By the end of term the pupils attended regularly and they were never late. This trend continued in the secondary school where the mentor kept a watching brief and encouraged the girls.
General fears about change	77 children worked in small groups of 6-7 and looked at specific issues about transfer that concerned them. Group work involved • group confidentiality • interaction with others • sharing ideas • participation • team-building • respect for others and their views	Many concerns were raised in a safe environment enabling children to share information, fears and problems, but also to find a solution within the group. The children also learned the importance of confidentiality, respect for one another and the importance of achieving something from meeting.
What will secondary school be like?	All the children in year 6 in two primary schools worked on The Big School book which looks at life in a secondary school. They worked in small groups and went through, in detail, any problems or concerns they felt they may face when they go to secondary school.	This was very successful in making all the pupils feel more confident about the huge change they were about to experience. The environment in which the discussions took place was safe and so the children felt they could ask questions or share concerns or fears that they had.
Visit to Kings Norton High School	The purpose of the visit was to familiarise the pupils with their new school, be introduced to the teachers and to interact with secondary school pupils at the time of day that held the most fear. Visits were for the morning in groups of 20 with a mixture of children from different schools.	All the pupils went on the visit and came away feeling more relaxed and confident about secondary school. They made new friends and all said they felt less apprehensive about September.

Table 8.1 *(Continued)*

Pen pal system	One pupil was the only pupil from her school coming to KNHS so she was matched with two pupils from another school. The pupils wrote to one another and were able to meet on the visit to the secondary school.	The three girls became good friends and were put together in the same tutor group in the secondary school making transition easier and alleviating fears.
Computer club	Computer clubs were established at two primary schools and using PowerPoint, created a magazine giving information about the secondary school.	ICT skills enhanced, but social and creative skills were also developed. Developed a good knowledge about the secondary school.
1–1 mentoring of year 7 pupils at Kings Norton High School	Pupils who were considered vulnerable were mentored at KNHS by mentors who were already known to them.	All pupils attending regularly at KNHS and starting to settle down well.
Small group work with year 7	Pupils with low self-esteem met in a small group and focused on • building friendships • communication skills • teamwork and also did artwork as a means of expression.	All mentees felt better able to cope with school life, and gained greater self-confidence. Enjoyed the artwork as a form of therapy.
Dance club at KNHS	Year 9 pupils ran a dance club for year 7 pupils. The year 7 pupils were able to build relationships with some year 9 pupils and were able to share concerns and make new friends. Year 9 pupils offered peer support.	The year 7 pupils performed at the KNHS Christmas Show. The self-esteem of the year 9 pupils was raised, and the year 7 pupils saw positive role models in the school.
School phobic	A pupil did not start at the secondary school. He did not want to participate in any introductory activities offered, and his parents seemed to support the child's attitude. The mentor had him in school at specific times and undertook work on likes and dislikes and friendships. Work was incorporated around arts and crafts in which the pupil had a particular interest. Parents were also given support. Mentor liaised closely with the Education Psychologist.	Pupil became more confident and within three weeks had joined two lessons per day. It became evident however that it was the parents who perhaps were the school phobics, and they wanted to teach him at home. Child stopped attending and parents taught him at home with support from Learning Mentor as an interim measure.

Kings Norton High School in Birmingham has attempted to address the issue of cross-phase transfer by employing three Learning Mentors, Nikki Rees, Jenni Ralph and Debby Whyborn, who work both in the partner primary schools and in the secondary school. This is funded by the EiC Action Zone (KNEAZ). Through their work in the primary schools they get to know the year 6 pupils and their parents and are able to identify those for whom the transfer will be problematic. They work in the primary schools from February to July and then all three are based in Kings Norton High School from September to February. During the summer holidays the year 5 and 6 children are invited to a series of activities at the High School. These include art, dance, sport and science, and the children can take part in taster sessions. This gives them a chance to familiarise themselves with the school and meet some of the teachers. It also means that there is a known point of contact at the school for any parents or children who have any concerns about the impending transfer.

Examples of aspects of the work of these Learning Mentors related to the transfer of pupils are summarised in Table 8.1.

The secondary school

Within secondary schools, Learning Mentors have to fit into what may be an elaborate staffing structure, as well as gaining staff support and understanding. Maggie Aylott, Deputy Headteacher at Dormers Wells High School in Southall, outlines how the role of the Learning Mentor has developed in the school.

> 'The Learning Mentors feel valued.' That statement might not have been true two years ago when the new profession began working in Dormers Wells High School. To a certain extent teachers did not understand the role of the new Learning Mentor and the Learning Mentor did not understand the extent of the input of teachers. There was a sense that traditional territory was being usurped.
>
> Dormers Wells High School always had a very effective pastoral system. With 55 per cent qualifying for free school meals, 55 per cent on the Special Needs Register, 82 per cent of the students not having English as their first language, a strong pastoral care system is vital. Year Managers supported by Deputy Year Managers work within Key Stages alongside a Deputy Head and Assistant Headteachers. This team, all teachers and including the Headteacher, has over the years developed counselling and mediation skills as well as an ability to administer rewards and sanctions fairly. Suddenly Learning Mentors seemed to be expected to take the counselling role, leaving only the traditional discipline role to the pastoral team. In addition, Learning Mentors often came from careers other than teaching, maybe a Social Worker, an Education Social Worker or Careers Adviser, and were initially asking more questions than they could answer.
>
> It is a testimony to both groups of staff that two years on, the teachers have a clear understanding that the students benefit from having a Learning Mentor and the Learning Mentors themselves feel that their work is valued.
>
> Our current Learning Mentor manager, Matthew Job feels that the school has worked

hard to develop processes to absorb the new profession so that it complements the extensive existing pastoral services. He feels that in other schools where there is not such a well-established pastoral provision, the Learning Mentors feel that they are working in a vacuum.

At Dormers Wells the Learning Mentors complement the work of the Year Manager and Deputy Year Manager, the SENCO, the school-based Education Social Worker, the Learning Support Centre Manager, the Gifted and Talented Co-ordinator and Excellence Challenge Co-ordinator, as well as external provision from the Ealing Youth Counselling and Information Service, the LEA Pre-exclusion team and the Educational Psychologist.

Matthew's Golden Rules for the new Learning Mentor role are

- to read up as much about the school and its existing support services as possible
- to read the DfES guidelines for Learning Mentors
- to understand the school's perception of the Learning Mentor role
- to make sure that the Leadership Team support Learning Mentors
- to communicate clearly and offer views, ideas and solutions
- to be innovative within school systems
- to get involved with a range of school activities – residentials, day trips, sporting activities
- to actively support the school's rewards and sanctions procedures.

Certainly Matthew's approach has rapidly changed what seemed like a bolt-on, rather peripheral service, which initially seemed to be operating within its own code of conduct, into a valued strand of the school's support services.
Joining in school social and extra-curricular activities has also helped forge the team feeling. Matthew plays in the school staff football team and finds that existing staff are quick to invite the Learning Mentors to social gatherings. He finds staff open and approachable. The Learning Mentors have helped on camping expeditions and in the organisation of Black History Month.

Perhaps the most successful events have been the school's focus evenings. These are now into their third year and were an innovation of the headteacher. In 2000 the headteacher identified that one strategy to improve parental liaison would be to run focus groups for identified groups of parents. Our first focus evening was for Somali parents and was hosted by the headteacher, aided by our first, single Learning Mentor. By the following focus evening for Somali parents the school had a team of three Learning Mentors who were key to the success of the evening through contacting parents by telephone and encouraging them to attend. The Learning Mentors maintained this role for the subsequent two focus evenings for parents of students of African-Caribbean heritage. At the focus evenings the Learning Mentors joined in the workshops, providing valuable input from both their professional and personal experiences.

Matthew reflects that there are differences between working as a Learning Mentor at Key Stage 3 and at Key Stage 4. In Key Stage 3 the Learning Mentor can spend more time with the students, whereas in Key Stage 4 contact is more generally restricted in an attempt to avoid disrupting the delivery of the GCSE curriculum. He feels that success is greater when his team are able to work with students as early as possible, modelling a positive and 'can do' culture.

Learning Mentors can provide an opportunity for students to discuss issues with someone who is not a teacher. Matthew feels that as a young, black male professional he can work with students and their parents and provide a good role model for them. He has an open management style and his team meet weekly to discuss the way forward and seek proactive solutions. Matthew meets with his line manager, the Key Stage 3 Deputy Head regularly. Learning Mentors attend a half-termly referral meeting which the school calls Interplan, where all the pastoral support teams meet and discuss who is best qualified to work with identified students. From this students are referred to SENPLAN where referrals to external agencies are made, and the Learning Mentors are also present at this meeting. Individual Learning Mentors are allocated to Year Teams and attend the Year Team meetings. The Learning Mentors provide half-termly reports for staff about their students.

The Learning Mentor team has grown from 1 to 3.5 with the associated problem of needing private interview space in a school where office and interview rooms are already at a premium. As it was a new profession there were inevitably teething troubles while Learning Mentors learnt about the school and the school explored the potential of Learning Mentors. Line managers worked hard to integrate the support system, and in two years Learning Mentors have become a valued part of school provision.

What about secondary school concerns?

Learning mentors in secondary schools tackle many of the same issues as their primary colleagues, but the experience of adolescence and the schools' drive to raise standards can cause the emphasis to change. There is inevitably a stress on developing good study habits, and supporting pupils to achieve the best that they can. Pupils with behaviour problems are often referred to the Learning Mentor both 'for their own good', and to enable the teacher to engage without disruption with the classes they are attempting to teach.

When secondary Learning Mentors were asked to identify their top reasons for referral, a great deal of commonality emerged, and the 'top ten'(not in rank order) emerged as:

- behaviour
- poor attendance
- underachievement
- bullying
- personal issues
- relationships
- social problems
- emotional support
- bereavement
- anger management.

Many of these issues have been addressed elsewhere in the book, but here we will give consideration to emotional literacy.

The statutory curriculum has an emphasis on development of skills and acquisition of knowledge, and little time is available for discussion and reflection. Learning Mentors need both to be able to help the children become more aware of themselves, and also to understand how to take the emotional life of the child into account when working with them. Many Learning Mentors are very skilled at helping the pupils develop greater self-awareness through relaxation, through encouraging pupils to talk about their feelings and through explaining them. Earlier in the chapter the use of meditation was discussed; other mentors use music as a stimulus, while others use a range of relaxation techniques.

Joan Eastman at Ninestiles Technology College in Birmingham regularly uses a range of techniques with the pupils to help them reflect on their feelings and has produced a booklet for the pupils outlining some of the techniques. Some extracts are reproduced in Figure 8.2. These different ideas are used to enable the pupils both to feel relaxed and, in turn, to feel more positive about themselves at the end of the experience. They are techniques that the children may take with them through life because once learned they are rarely forgotten.

Such experiences enable the children to use their emotional experiences to bring back the 'feel good factor' at times when they most need it – when they are under stress. It allows the children the opportunity to remove their negative emotions that are associated with, for example, low self-esteem, anger, uncertainty. These are just the first steps in dealing with emotional intelligence, and Learning Mentors should take time to research and find out more about the need for pupils to be 'emotionally literate'. Pupils who have experienced support in developing this are most definitely more inclined to be:

- happier and more relaxed
- in control
- empathetic
- more considerate of others
- able to problem-solve difficult situations

Study skills and time management in Key Stage 4

Schools are under pressure to constantly improve their performance, and the external evidence of this is performance in national tests, especially GCSE. Schools are compared according to their performance in relation to, for example the percentage of pupils achieving A*–C grades, or percentages achieving at least 5 A*–G grades. This has on the positive side led to discussions about the nature of learning and scrutiny of assessment, but a negative consequence has been a stress on A*–C grades, which has tended to negate the efforts of those who really work hard to achieve lower grades, but which represent excellent grades for them.

Under the Excellence in Cities initiative Gifted and Talented Co-ordinators have been employed to enable youngsters who are identified as being gifted to attain as well as they possibly can. Some Learning Mentors work alongside the Gifted and

CIRCLE OF EXCELLENCE

Identify a feeling such as being confident or happy

Imagine a circle on the floor. This represents that state of excellence. Imagine it has a colour.

Remember an actual time when you had that feeling. Take a deep breath.

Step into the memory inside the circle. Relive it and strengthen the feelings you had.

Stop. Step out of the circle and shake …

POSITIVE LISTINGS

Make a list of at least 10 occasions when you have felt good about yourself or when something really good has happened.

....
....
....

Add to this list every day

RELAXATION …

Get into a comfortable sitting or lying position in a quiet place

Focus on your breathing

Ensure your stomach moves out when you breathe in

Notice the rhythm of your breathing

POWERFUL ANCHORS

Think of a time in the future when you would like to be more successful.

Identify your feelings for this situation. Remember the experience and imagine you are there, noticing – what you see, what you hear, what you feel.

Break concentration on the memory. Use something simple like noticing the colour on the carpet.

Select your anchor – this is a physical act such as clenching your fist or squeezing a knuckle.

Go back to the start of the exercise and relive it, strengthening the emotions and feelings. Practice until firing the anchor brings back the positive feelings automatically …

Figure 8.2 Reflecting on feelings

Talented Co-ordinators and support them in their work of raising their aspirations.

More commonly, however, Learning Mentors become involved in opportunities to help the pupils develop their study and organisational skills. The students have a heavy burden of work as they embark on their external examination courses, and right from the start of year 10 they need to have an overview of important deadlines during years 10 and 11. It is also important that they understand the methods of assessment being employed in their courses.

Coursework is a general term used to describe work which is assessed as part of an examination, but does not involve a written test. The marks obtained for coursework go towards the final GCSE exam grade. Types of work which count as coursework are:

- assignments in English, history, religious education
- fieldwork in geography
- practical/project work in art, maths, technology, science
- composition in music
- performance in PE, drama.

The purpose of coursework is to test a wider range of skills than is possible in final written exams. Skills which are tested include

- researching
- working in groups
- making accurate records and using powers of observation
- planning and organising a long piece of work
- using apparatus and machinery
- communication
- investigation, planning, design.

Percentage of marks awarded for coursework varies with different subjects; for example, in geography it is 25 per cent. Learning Mentors can help the students better cope with the pressures of this type of assessment through breaking the worries into small manageable pieces. The following are some examples of typical concerns.

Problem	Some suggestions
Getting started	Start at a time when you are feeling alert and pick out some aspects of the work that you find particularly interesting. Make a plan for your work.
Motivating yourself	Think about what you want to achieve – getting good marks for coursework reduces pressure when it comes to the final exam.
Presentation	Present your work as neatly as possible and use a variety of techniques, e.g. drawings, photographs, diagrams, pictures if appropriate. Start off with an interesting front page and a contents page, etc.
Keeping deadlines	Make a timetable on which deadlines are clearly marked for all subjects for which you have coursework. Set targets and keep to them.

The same principle can be applied to work during the two years of the GCSE courses, and it is helpful to have an overview of assessments over the two years so that pressure points can be identified early on and appropriate support be put in place (see figure 8.3). In addition to support with organisation and study support, many Learning Mentors offer various types of help with relaxation and stress reduction.

	MONTH	IMPORTANT DATES TO REMEMBER
YEAR 10	September	An exciting time – new subjects, new teachers
	October	Review your performance in all subjects – are you up to date with work in all subjects ? If not, why not?
	November	First English assignment due in.
	December	Review your progress this term – what have you done well and enjoyed? What do you need help with? Who can help you?
	January	
	February	Geography fieldwork trip – then coursework to be started
	March	
	April	Make a revision timetable for your year 10 exams
	May	
	June	End of year exams
	July	Work experience
	August	Have a good holiday but don't forget your coursework
YEAR 11	September	New term – new year – new start
	October	Half term study support sessions for English and maths
	November	
	December	Trial/mock examinations
	January	Start planning your revision NOW
	February	Half term revision sessions
	March	Easter holidays – study support sessions in all subjects
	April	
	May	Examinations start
	June	

Join our lunchtime relaxation classes

Figure 8.3 Overview of assessment work

Alternative curriculum provision

There are pupils for whom the Key Stage 4 curriculum has little to offer. While some pupils just settle down and get on with it, others actively reject it and for example start to take time off school or exhibit poor behaviour or become demotivated. If some type of intervention is not put in place, these pupils are in danger of self-exclusion from the education process. Figure 8.4 shows some options which are available to the Learning Mentor. Some schools employ Leaning Mentors to specialise in this aspect of the work, for if support is to be effective for these youngsters this is a very time-consuming role.

Brookfield High School in Kirkby, Knowsley, is an 11–16 co-education community comprehensive which is also a specialist sports college. It serves an area where youth unemployment is over 30 per cent, very few people have a higher education qualification and approximately a quarter of the population aged 16-60 have low or very low literacy and numeracy skills. The school is committed to improving the lives of the young people and their community by promoting high achievement and learning, developing self-confidence, self-belief and self-esteem. This commitment applies as much to those who are in danger of opting out as to the academic high fliers.

Robbie Holmes is the Learning Mentor responsible for co-ordinating the school's alternative curriculum provision, which is called the 'Preparation for Work and Training Programme'. This involves the organisation of a thoroughly planned programme and oversight of pupils at the local college or training provider. The pupils are carefully selected and are interviewed by the college liaison officer prior to the confirmation of a place. The programme is so popular and successful with pupils that demand always outweighs the number of places available.

The programme is flexible to enable each young person to have an individual timetable. Courses offered include hairdressing, motor vehicle maintenance, ICT and construction at the local further education college or at training providers. The programme also includes

- A day's work experience each week with local employers
- Personal mentoring
- Individual action planning
- A basic skills package either on or off the school site
- The opportunity to take part in a range of activities such as climbing, canoeing and performing arts.

The pupils who participate in the programme make excellent progress, and attendance at college and in school improve significantly as they become motivated to learn. In some instances for the first time, the pupils enjoy their education, learn more independently, take greater responsibility for their own work and show a very mature attitude both in college and in school. All the pupils complete their own action plan for their selected course and meet with staff regularly to monitor their own progress. As a result they have a very clear knowledge of how well they are achieving and seek to improve their own performance. Robbie considers that the

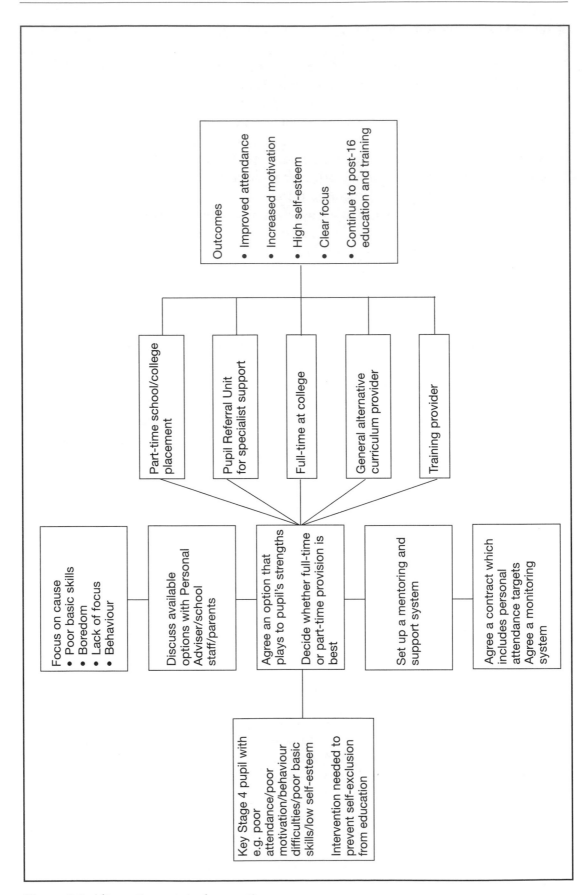

Figure 8.4 Alternative curriculum options

following are key to the success of the programme:

- Constant support for the young people
- Regular monitoring of attendance
- Regular communication with parents and gaining their support – essential
- Close liaison with the colleges, employers and agencies involved
- Weekly visits to the agencies to show support for the students
- A portfolio for each student to provide evidence of achievement
- Maintaining the motivation of the students through regular mentoring sessions to help them to reflect on and explore aims
- Ensuring college and schoolwork is up to date; liaising with teachers, the attendance team and college
- Empowering the young people to take responsibility for themselves.

Post-16 transitions

Learning Mentors are involved in supporting Key Stage 4 students as they are making decisions about their next steps into post-16 education, training or work. Much of this involves raising their aspiration and broadening their horizons and providing them with facts about opportunities available to them. As the mentors are likely to be working with youngsters who lack confidence, they will also need support with the actual processes of completing application forms, visiting colleges and work placements and attending interviews. There are some aspects which are best left to the expertise of the Connexions Personal Advisers who will have contacts in the local colleges and training providers and be familiar with what is on offer. They can also continue to support the pupils once they have left school. Learning Mentors and Personal Advisers can also beneficially work together – listed below are some examples of successful joint working:

School A
- The Learning Mentor contacts young people who are chronic non-attenders and encourages them to come into school to meet the Personal Adviser
- The Learning Mentor and Personal Adviser work together to identify and find alternative provision to meet client needs
- Learning Mentor gives good support to the Personal Adviser in finding out the destination of school leavers

School B
- The Learning Mentor and Personal Adviser attend in-school Connexions family meeting which includes pastoral staff and attendance officer
- Learning Mentor and Personal Adviser share ideas on how to support individual pupils
- Learning Mentor and Personal Adviser work jointly on projects, e.g. 4Real and Flexibility in Learning

School C
- Learning Mentor and Personal Adviser work jointly on 14-16 Learning Gateway, e.g. joint interviews and reviews
- Learning Mentor and Personal Adviser share information on individual students, identify possible problems and their solutions
- Make joint referrals to trainers and alternative provision
- Share information on useful contacts

All of the examples given in this chapter are a credit to the mentors who gave us their time, and without whom, this chapter would not have been possible. Their dedication was apparent throughout as they spoke about their work with enthusiasm, passion and genuine affection for the children in their care.

Our final chapter leads us towards the conclusion of the book, but it is by no means any less important. As we look towards the developing role of the Learning Mentors we must consider the importance of their continuing professional development.

9 Training, networking and the way ahead

Learning Mentors are making a tremendous impact on schools and on the youngsters with whom they come into contact. The NFER evaluation confirms that Learning Mentors have been well received by pupils and teachers and that nearly three-quarters of teachers felt that all pupils should have access to a trained mentor. The evaluation further states, however, that some initial concern has been voiced about the selection, pay, training and role of Learning Mentors, and how they relate to teachers and teaching. This certainly became apparent during meetings and discussions with some of the mentors while writing this book. It is from here therefore that we begin to consider the current picture, the way forward and the whole issue surrounding continuing professional development.

One of the strengths of Learning Mentors is that they come from a variety of backgrounds and bring with them a wealth of experience. Many of them may have come into the role from non-educational settings. Even those who have educational backgrounds need to consider that they are undertaking a completely different role from any previously experienced. In light of this there are many different needs as far as individual training and professional development are concerned.

Five-day national training

As a matter of course, all mentors have access to the five-day National Training Programmes. The Primary Learning Mentors' training programme was developed by the Liverpool Excellence Partnership and includes four modules:

1 The Primary School as a Learning Organisation
2 The Role of the Primary Learning Mentor
3 The Nature of Children's Learning
4 Supporting Children and Families

The Secondary Learning Mentors' training programme was developed by the Association of Colleges and Rotherham College of Arts and Technology. It has been developed as a two-day block followed by three separate training days. Each LEA is offered the menu of six modules that are outlined below. From these they are able to formulate three one-day events.

1 Use of counselling skills to identify barriers to learning
2 Personal effectiveness in working with others
3 Managing behaviour in order to raise achievement
4 Group work in raising achievement
5 Culture and equal opportunities in addressing barriers to learning
6 Strategies and skills in ensuring effective monitoring and evaluation

Accreditation is available through portfolio, ranging from level 2 and up to units towards Masters programmes.

Self-directed learning

In addition to the above, the *Learning Mentor Manual* is a reference manual from which Learning Mentors can get advice and information on specific issues. It also serves as a self-directed learning pack for use by newly appointed Learning Mentors, and the exercises contained within the manual help the Learning Mentor to build up a portfolio of evidence to achieve accreditation via the NVQ network. The manual covers six units :

1 Introduction to the Learning Mentor role
2 An Introduction to the Education System
3 The Learning Mentor and School
4 Learning Mentor–Pupil Relationships
5 Monitoring and Evaluation
6 Further Development

Additional help is available from the DfES *Good Practice Guidelines for Learning Mentors* (2001), which includes a cross-reference to their website examples of good practice. It is regarded by most Learning Mentors as their initial reference source should they require guidance. Many of these examples of good practice have been customised and used by individual schools, and the willingness of schools to so freely share such good practice is certainly a strength of networking among Learning Mentors.

In addition to all of this there is a further training need that requires consideration. This relates to the Learning Mentor's working situation. All schools are different and for each mentor there will be specific training required to support them in their role.

Accessing support

In an earlier chapter, we mentioned the need for a senior member of staff in the school to familiarise the Learning Mentor with aspects of school routines and organisation. In addition to this there are also issues that are specific to the Learning Mentor's role that have to be addressed. Where there is more than one Learning Mentor in the school, this is relatively easy to arrange, but where there is only one

Learning Mentor outside help will most definitely be needed. This may come from the Link Learning Mentor or from the many networks that exist within the Excellence in Cities Partnership. Schools and mentors will need to consider the areas that they wish to cover to enable effective practice to take place, but they most certainly should include:

• An introduction to external agencies that work with the school, especially those who are responsible for attendance, behaviour support, health and home–school liaison
• An awareness of volunteer mentoring groups
• An awareness of those who have responsibility for child protection and children who are looked after within the school
• How to work with individuals and small groups, including circle time and dealing with issues such as anger management
• How to action plan and target set
• How to write reports and case studies
• An awareness of both the social and economic nature of the community around the school
• Access to links with other Learning Mentors both informally and more formally through local Learning Mentor networks and cluster groups.

Specialised training

As Learning Mentors become more familiar with their roles, many may wish to undertake further professional training. It may be that some degree of specialist knowledge is required to provide specific types of support to individuals or groups. There may be the need to further develop greater understanding in areas where some knowledge has already been acquired. It may be that they wish to undertake new initiatives. Whatever the reason, mentors should be openly encouraged by their schools and local education authorities to further their professional development by allowing them access to training.

Where to access the training

Learning Mentors will need to enquire how to access courses that meet their identified training need. We would suggest that in the first instance enquiring within their school via the person responsible for professional development would be a good start. In addition to this, other Learning Mentors within the LEA, and access to mentor websites, may equally be good sources of information.

As the role of the mentor develops there will most certainly be an increase in the range and number of courses available to them as training providers become more aware of their needs. There are already some training providers who are able to offer courses that focus upon particular areas of work that would most definitely support the Learning Mentor in carrying out their role. They have experience of supporting teachers and other workers who are involved with those pupils who have become disengaged from learning.

One such provider is an organisation called Evita, whose main focus is to share good practice. They describe themselves in the following way:

> Evita is the not-for-profit training arm of the Birmingham Village Partnership and draws on the experience of staff working daily with difficult and disaffected young people and their families.

Part of the training they provide focuses on those areas that are often problematic to youngsters who have become, or are in danger of becoming, disaffected. They offer a range of training and workshops on topics that include

- Effective communication
- Self-esteem
- Active listening
- Children affected by loss or trauma
- Anger management.

This type of training will most certainly be of value to Learning Mentors in their day-to-day work within schools and most definitely add to their overall expertise. Mentors who wish to access such training can do so through the Birmingham Village Partnership, based at Lyndsworth School.

Training others

As a part of their role, Learning Mentors may themselves be involved in training others. In Sheffield, for example, a Learning Mentors' Education Support Programme (Peer Mentoring and Study Skills) has been written by Julia Baker for use by Learning Mentors. It consists of two modules, and each module is accredited by the Open College Network at three levels. The modules are designed to be used in educational settings to provide a framework for supporting students and adults working in schools in a variety of ways. The programme can address particular issues and provide national accreditation and qualifications through the Open College Network. A range of people, including Learning Mentors and Personal Advisers, have been trained to deliver the programme, and it has been used to train students, parents and business and volunteer mentors.

Schools who get involved in the programme have access to support and advice in setting up the programme, as well as ongoing support to ensure successful implementation of the programme.

Details for the mentoring module are outlined in Figure 9.1, and further details about this and the study skills module may be obtained by contacting Julia Baker.

	Module 1	*Module 2*	*Module 3*
Title	Peer Mentoring	Mentoring Skills	Mentoring Skills
Accreditation	OCN level 1	OCN level 2	OCN level 3
Target Group	<ul><li>Student Peer Mentors</li><li>Prefect training</li><li>Personal Development for disaffected students</li><li>Accredited framework for existing group work activities (e.g. attendance groups) to help and encourage peer support</li></ul>	<ul><li>Student Peer Mentors</li><li>Prefect training</li><li>Enrichment for Gifted and Talented and Widening Participation students</li><li>Business and Volunteer Mentors</li></ul>	<ul><li>FE/HE Mentors</li><li>Volunteer and Business Mentors</li></ul>

Figure 9.1 Mentoring modules

The role of Link Learning Mentors in relation to professional development

The Link Learning Mentors have an important part to play in supporting the professional development of Learning Mentors. They are instrumental in maintaining contacts between Learning Mentors in Partnership areas and for disseminating information. They work directly with the mentors but also liaise with the senior managers in schools with regard to the work of mentors and report on training to the Partnership.

Regular training is provided through network meetings with mentors. Agendas for the meetings are usually planned in response to needs of the mentors and could include topics such as bullying, the work of the school nurse, needs of 'Looked After' children or emotional literacy. Good practice is shared and concerns raised. Link Learning Mentors also offer support through regular 'Drop In' sessions and of course undertake individual visits to support mentors in schools. Cluster group meetings also provide the opportunity for exchange of information between schools. They also keep the mentors informed about training opportunities, including those that are accredited. Link Learning Mentors are able to sustain links with school Learning Mentors through establishing websites to share information and good practice.

Status of Learning Mentors

The only thing that Learning Mentors have in common is their title. Their roles are developed to meet the unique needs of their schools. All Learning Mentors are appointed by headteachers and governors and are part of the school staff. Common agreement exists about salary levels and contracts, and a pay and career structure is reflected in the appointment of Assistant Learning Mentors as well as Learning Mentors, but in reality a range of contracts exist within schools. At one end of the spectrum are Learning Mentors who are members of the Senior Management Team while at the other are Learning Mentors who are still struggling to be accepted by the teaching staff.

Some Learning Mentors may have a 52-week contract, which takes account of holiday activities and out-of-hours working, while others may be term-time only or paid on a pro rata basis.

Whatever their status, it is essential that Learning Mentors have an opportunity to keep staff informed about their work. This can be done through, for example, their attendance at meetings, through contributions to staff briefings and through school newsletters on a regular basis, but there is also a need for the staff to have a formal input about the nature of the work of the Learning Mentor. Conflict has been known to occur when the class teacher does not fully understand the role of the Learning Mentor and criticises them for not doing something which was not their responsibility anyway. It is here perhaps where schools need to consider staff training to enable them to fully understand the role of the Learning Mentor within their school. Where limited understanding exists Learning Mentors will struggle to be fully effective. In light of this, as we come to the conclusion of the book, perhaps it is time to reflect on the work of the Learning Mentors in our schools and consider the way forward.

The way forward

As we have seen from the NFER evaluation mentioned earlier in this chapter and from the many examples cited throughout the book, excellent work is being done by an ever increasing number of mentors in schools. It is vital that as their role develops and as the impact of their work becomes more widely spread every effort is made to ensure that their role is truly valued. In order to achieve this, schools, LEAs and the Partnerships must look towards the continued development of the professional working relationship between mentors, their schools and beyond. As a part of that, their terms and conditions of working and access to continued professional development is surely a must.

As we finally draw to a close, we would like to take this opportunity to reiterate what the book has hopefully shown – that Learning Mentors have provided and are providing a wonderful support mechanism to some of the most challenging and challenged children in our schools. Long may they continue…

Bibliography

Department of Education (1994) *Bullying: Don't Suffer in Silence.*

Department for Education and Employment (1999) *Social Inclusion: The LEA Role in Pupil Support* (Circular 11/99).

Department for Education and Employment (2000) *Removing the Barriers* (DfEE Guidance 0012/000).

Department for Education and Employment (2000) *Guidance on the Education of Young People in Public Care.*

Department for Education and Skills (2001) *Good Practice Guidelines for Learning Mentors.*

Department for Education and Skills (2001) *Special Educational Needs Code of Practice.*

Department for Education and Skills (2002) *Good Practice Guide on the Education of Asylum Seeking and Refugee Children.*

Excellence in Cities *Learning Mentor Handbook*

Gillborn, D., and Mirza, H. S. (2000) *Education Inequality: Mapping Race, Class and Gender.* Ofsted.

Graham, P., and Hughes, C. (1995) *So Young, So Sad, So Listen*, Gaskell and West London Health Promotion Agency.

Mental Health Foundation (1999) *Bright Futures: Promoting Children and Young People's Mental Health*, Mental Health Foundation.

NAPCE (1997) *Death and Bereavement*, National Association for Pastoral Care in Education.

NFER (2002) *Evaluation of Excellence in Cities: Overview of Interim Findings*, National Foundation for Education Research.

Ofsted *The Education of Travelling Children.*

Ofsted *Raising Achievement of Children in Public Care.*

Social Exclusion Unit (1999) *Report on Teenage Pregnancy.*

The Children Act 1989.

Additional reading

Beere, J. (2002) *The Key Stage 3 Learning Kit*, Connect Publications.

Burnett, G. (2002) *Learning to Learn*, Crown House Publishing.

Krupska, M., and Klein, C. (1995) *Demystifying Dyslexia*, London Language and Literacy Unit.

Relf, P., Hirst, R., Richardson, J., and Youdell, G. (1998) *Best Behaviour*, Network Educational Press.

Rowan, Dr P. (1998) *Big Head*, The Bodley Head, London.

Smith, Alistair (1996) *Accelerated Learning in the Classroom*, Network Educational Press.

Weatherley, C. (2000) *Leading the Learning School*, Network Educational Press.

Index

How to order from David Fulton Publishers

If you have found this book useful and you are interested in ordering any of the other titles listed below please contact us or use this order form.
Just photocopy this page and send it to:

David Fulton Publishers, The Chiswick Centre, 414 Chiswick High Road, London W4 5TF

Alternatively you can telephone, fax, email or order online:

Freecall: 0500 618052   Fax: +44 (0) 020 8996 3622

E-mail: orders@fultonpublishers.co.uk   on-line: www.fultonpublishers.co.uk

ORDER FORM

Qty	ISBN	Title	Price
	1-85346-825-8	How to Raise Boysí Achievement	£15.00
	1-85346-775-8	Improving Behaviour and Raising Self-Esteem in the Classroom	£15.00
	1-85346-678-6	Nurturing Emotional Literacy	£17.00
	1-85346-834-7	Sex and Relationships Education	£15.00
	1-85346-764-2	Supporting Children with Behaviour Difficulties	£14.00

Payment

☐   By credit card (Visa / Access / Mastercard / American Express / Switch / Delta)

☐   By cheque with order. Please make cheques payable to David Fulton Publishers Ltd.

☐   With invoice (applicable to schools, LEAs and other institutions)

Postage and Packing: £2.50 for up to 2 books plus 50p for each additional book. Maximum carriage charge is £8.00.

Credit card number

Expiry date   (Switch customers only) valid from   issue number

Name	Order No./Ref
Position	Date

School/LEA/Company

Address

Postcode

Telephone Number	Signature

4358